# Marbles

ONCE UPON A TIME (1980) in a land far far away called 5 Scott Drive, my older brother Jerry sent me a small wooden vertical sign with the Japanese 'kanji' that phonetically represented 'Biederman'.

**He suggested that the word 'Bie' could mean 'beauty' in Japanese.**

They clearly use a different alphabet. Spelling becomes irrelevant so long as the pronunciation sounds like the first syllable of our name.

**The word 'der' is a Japanese word that could mean 'peace',**

**... and 'man' could mean 'full' or 'fullness'.**

Saying 'Biederman' in Japanese you could be saying the three Japanese words that mean 'beauty', 'peace' and 'full'. It can get more complex due to the large number of homonyms in the Japanese language.

'Biederman', spoken as one word rather than three, means 'marbles'. But who wants a name like *Marbles*?

Copyright © 2014 by Robert Biederman
Published by Robert Biederman
1500 East Ocean Boulevard  Suite #407
Long Beach, CA 90802
www.robertbiederman.com

Library of Congress control # 2013920751
ISBN: 978-0-9910738-0-1

Printed in the United States of America.
*Dedicated to Emma* was previously published by the *Boston* Globe on July 4, 2005. Reprinted with permission.
*Casey's Diner* was previously published by The *MetroWest Daily News* on May 14, 2003. Reprinted with permission.

**Cover design by compu-vison.**
**Book design and layout by compu-vison.**
**www.compu-vision.com.au**

**Credits**
*Daughter* was cowritten by Lisa Maddock.
*Granddaughter* was written by Emma Flowers.

**Name changes**
Some names have been changed in the following chapters
to protect the privacy of those involved: *Tip Time*, *Kevin*, and *Frank*.
You can believe just about all the rest except where indicated.

# marbles
## frontiers of mor*(t)*ality

Bob Biederman et.al.

# Letter to an editor

Dear Tetra,

Enclosed find a check in the amount of $194 for 'balance due' for your editorial services. I admit that when I hired you it was partly because your first name sounded a bit Greek and I was hoping for a *Homeric* quality to your literary advice. Instead, I got a few notes on proper syntax and inconsistent verb tense. I felt like I got the other uncomfortable and unsavory Greek experience.

When I sent you the $200 advance, we agreed that your job was to help me make clear to my reader that the title, **Marbles: Frontiers of Mor(t)ality**, means that each of the twenty-one stories focuses on those moments in our lives when we're faced with our mortality: life or death. That's when we make tough moral decisions. They affect our closest relations and have consequences that test our morality and shape our lives. How do we make this plain to the reader? It wasn't about proper use of gerund phrases or the pluperfect.

Your further help is not needed and, by the way, I ignored your advice to delete the two pieces that had sexual content. I know you felt that they might offend a female reader. Quite frankly, there are females in the world that aren't so overstuffed with estrogen that they have no room for a little sense of humor in there. The first example is likely to elicit a grin and a wink. If not, that's their problem. The second may be a bit unsettling to some, but I'll play my "Get out of jail free" card and hope for their forgiveness. After all, if my wife can forgive me, so can they.

Cordially,
BB


Enc: $194.00

# Table d'hôte

# Preface

I AM FOREVER A SON trying to learn the lessons of fatherhood
and hoping my own son will be a better father than me.
And You? Is there a more important task in your life?
Is parenthood the ultimate test of your own morality?
How do you behave when facing the edges of mortality?

# TIP time

## Surviving on the frontier

HOW DO YOU SHOOT yourself twice?

That's what the two slugs retrieved from the floorboard and ceiling indicated. That's what the bloody footprints said.

Fifteen-year-old Darren had come home from school to find his eighteen-year-old brother, Sean, on the bathroom floor, dead from a self-inflicted gunshot wound to the face. The fifteen-year-old, who was with his grandmother, 'lost it' and ran screaming from the house. The grandmother was a strong lady who did what she could.

Conflicting details made the circumstances of this death bizarre. They just made no sense, not that any suicide does. It seemed that Sean had shot himself in the midsection first, while sitting on the toilet. He didn't quite kill himself, so he walked into his father's bedroom, got another gun, went back into the bathroom, and finished the job with a shot aimed upward, beneath his chin.

My name is Bob. I'm a TIP volunteer. This is what I encounter.

## ... marbles ...

The Trauma Intervention Program was created to deal with the 'Second Injury' victims, those people closest to the trauma victim whom nobody has time for. There wasn't much to be done for the deceased, but the brother, grandmother, and parents were now in harm's way from the emotional trauma they were dealing with. My job is to protect them from *the system*, well-meaning but toxic friends, and themselves.

This was a very tragic and convoluted situation. I arrived at the condominium complex in Reading, Massachusetts, on a midsummer afternoon. The light rain had stopped. Flashing police lights led me to the scene, where I stepped under the yellow police tape connected to the three-level clapboard buildings. They were painted a bright yellow with green trim and had attractive window boxes of peonies and purple and green coleus. Adolescent shrubs below that marked it as a recently built upper middle-class community.

The air was damp and misty. I decided to focus on the father, who stood like a large stone in the street. As soon as I saw him, I knew where he really was.

Physically he stood in the middle of the cul-de- sac with his hands jammed in his jeans, shoulders hunched, head down. I approached him as I was trained.

"Hello, Michael, I'm Bob from the Trauma Team. I'm here to help get you through this night."

No recognition, response, or acknowledgment. I took three steps back and gave him space. He had heard my voice. I was sure of that. What was there to say in response? Somehow I had to enter that small little room he was in. The one with no windows or doors. The darkness. The silence with only an echo of your own thoughts – bad thoughts.

But how?

The only tools right now were patience, my Trauma Intervention Program training, and the dozen calls I had already been on in the last five months.

I shadowed Michael from about five to ten yards for most of the call. For me it would last seven hours and forty-five minutes. It was the second call of my twelve-hour shift that would make this a nineteen-hour day. One of three I spend each month. It was unusual, but not unexpected.

"Every call is different," we were told. "You'll never know what you'll find when you get to the scene. Listen to the First Responders. Ask questions and observe."

TIP volunteers go through nearly sixty hours of intensive training over a two-week period, with nearly two hundred pages of collateral readings done as homework. We're well oriented to *the system*. We know what the police need to do and what they want us to do so they can be more effective. We know what the firefighters need to do, the paramedics, and the coroner. In fact, in cases of death (80 percent of our calls involve a death), the coroner is in charge of the scene and the body of the deceased. All of the municipal employees have their jobs. But no job includes looking after the emotional health of the Second Victim: the spouse, parent, or sibling of the deceased; the neighbor who witnessed the death, or the close family friend who may have been godmother to the deceased.

When you are witness to a traumatic death or have close ties to the deceased, you suffer some level of PTSD (post-traumatic stress disorder). It's not always immediately apparent, not always crippling, but it's always there. One human being does not witness the sudden traumatic death of another without its having a resounding psychological echo. Those reverberations must be dealt with in the most caring and efficient way to enable the Second Victim to survive the incident with the minimal amount of psychological damage. TIP volunteers are trained to understand and recognize what is going on in the minds of these second victims and to provide the emotional first aid necessary to get them back in touch with reality, their responsibilities, and their loved ones that remain.

The father, Michael Logan, had not spoken to his current wife. She was there at the scene. He had not spoken to his first wife, Sean's mother. She was there also and being helped by Sarah, my TIP partner. Michael had not spoken to his son, Darren, who had discovered his brother, Sean. Michael was not speaking to his own mother either.

He was just standing straight, shoulders a bit hunched with that stare. Eyes wet. While shadowing him, I also engaged the wife, the son to a limited degree, the grandmother, aunt, uncle, cousin, and Sean's mother, who had also arrived. It was another rather disjointed family.

Michael was four years into his second marriage. The information I gathered told me that he was a recovering alcoholic who had been suicidal when he was drinking, but he was three years sober. His father had been extremely abusive during his childhood until the father killed himself. Sean, the deceased son, had been a brilliant kid who hadn't seemed to fit in well socially and couldn't figure out why. He had just been kicked out of high school a month before, enrolled in a new high school, and kicked out again after just four days. He'd had a lovely girlfriend. There were many signs of suicide potential, but too many conflicting things that would contradict that. I just don't know.

I saw that Michael was in serious trouble and spoke to the police about it. They recognized it and removed the other guns from the house. I spoke with Michael's mother (the grand-mother), and she recognized it too. He clearly blamed himself and was emotionally locked in that small dark room. During the first two to three hours, I got Michael to respond to me through a few very simple requests, such as the retrieval of keys.

The police officer in charge of the crime scene called me over and told me that they were removing the guns from the house, and they would fill out the paperwork required to show their responsibility for the property. I was to tell Michael. I nodded and approached him from an angle, as we were trained.

"The police want you to know that they are taking custody of your two guns and are filling out all the paperwork needed so you know where they are and how to retrieve them."

"What?" a strong challenge.

"Why are they taking my guns?" a tinge of panic. Hazel eyes with pupils constricted focused on me. Still a handsome if pained face. We were engaged. And so it began.

"The officer didn't give me a full explanation of why. He just described the two guns and the ammunition and wanted me to tell you what they are doing."

"Why? Why are they taking my guns? What paperwork? I want to know why they are taking my guns and what paperwork they mean."

"I'll go and get the officer and have him talk directly to you. Will you stay right here?"

"Yes. I want to talk to the officer. I want to know why they are taking my guns."

Part of our training directs us to provide as much information as we can to our clients – accurate, simple, and responsive. When at all possible, we connect them with the professional who has that information, be it the police, the fire chief, or the ER physician. Clear, concise communication with no chance of misinterpretation. We facilitate communication. We try not to pass on secondhand summaries.

It was midevening now, around 8 PM. The police officer walked with me through the shadows to where Michael was standing just outside the glow of the streetlight. It was a midsummer night with fairly mild temperatures. Michael was wearing long sleeves, but looked a bit cold.

"Michael, this is Officer Bellflower. Can I get you a blanket?"

"Why are you taking my guns? What are you doing with them?"

As the officer began his response, I stepped back out of the halo of the street lamp and listened to what I could. The officer went over the paperwork and responded in a calm way to Michael's pained queries. He went over some things twice. Michael seemed to understand, if not agree. Officer Bellflower moved away, expressing his sincere sympathy to Michael, and nodded to me. I moved back a bit closer to Michael, in his peripheral arc of sight. There began some body language that indicated he accepted my being there as I followed along with him, not in his face, just in sight.

I spoke again with his mother, the grandmother who had discovered her grandson's body. She reminded me very much of a junior high school principal – strong, tough, no-nonsense, but with a guarded sensitivity accustomed to being in charge. She had told me a great deal about Michael and his difficult childhood and what an abusive beast his father had been before he killed himself. She seemed to express a balance of remorse and relief in describing that period. Now she was very worried about Michael.

We acknowledged the obvious danger of his taking his own life. She asked me to help him.

"What are you going to do?"

Without too much thought, I responded that "we" needed to help him. What could we do?

She had asked him repeatedly where he was going to stay that night. We had been in the street all this time because the home was a crime scene and they couldn't go back in, not that they ever would have wanted to. Scorsese minimizes the blood spilled in his violent deaths. A theater audience would not accept the gore of reality. Michael would never live in this home again. He would not respond to his mother's question other than with a shake of his head. His wife had asked the same question with the same response. This was a man who wasn't thinking about where his bed was going to be that night. Or maybe that's all he was thinking about. The grandmother was not giving up. We were a team.

"His son Darren needs him," she said. And that was my answer.

That was the strategy. Darren was planning to go home with his aunt and her family, where he had actually been staying for the previous few months. It had something to do with his school district and not wanting to change in midterm. His cousin, who was about his age, was with him this night, and they had been pretty much inseparable, except when the police had to question Darren about what he had seen. Darren was an extremely fragile teenager who had been emotionally shattered that afternoon.

My TIP partner on this call was Sarah, a middle-aged woman who had experienced a suicide in her own family. She was more skilled at dealing with children. During the course of the call, we had formed a tacit agreement as to who would concentrate on which victims. We each had contact with all of them, but she was clearly better at working with the children and the distraught mother while I focused on the father and the grandmother. We each worked with the other family members to a limited degree through the night. Working as a team isn't easy or always successful. This night it was. We had no conflict and had a complementary intuitive sense of what needed to be done.

One of the key ingredients in our TIP training is the strategy of distraction and redirection. If our clients seem likely to do something that would be injurious to themselves or others, we are instructed not to argue with them about their choice but just to help them reprioritize. In a gang shooting, there might be a primary urge to retaliate, to go out and get the guy that did it. We are told to point out that "Right now, your family needs you here. There's time for everything, but right now you need to help your mother (or brother or other grieving family member)." Don't argue, just redirect and reprioritize.

"Darren needs him," the grandmother had said. And that was the redirection. It was just past 9 PM. I approached Michael again, but this time at an oblique angle from the rear. He could see me coming, but not directly at him. I wanted to be physically close to him without being confrontational.

When I was standing about two feet from his left shoulder, I said, "Michael, Darren needs you tonight."

His head moved just a fraction in a kind of foggy acknowledgment. I stood silently. He did not respond further. I stayed closer than I had been and remained silent but present. I did not go more than six feet from him for about the next twenty minutes. He seemed to be moving away from me. He walked slowly around in the courtyard of the condominium complex.

A neighbor came up to express her sympathy. Michael was

nonresponsive at first, but then lifted his head and said. "Can I use your bathroom?"

He seemed to have a goal in his eyes. I felt uncomfortable.

"Certainly, Michael. Right inside the door. You know where it is, just the same as your house," the neighbor replied.

I felt a little yellowish red pain in my stomach. I couldn't follow him in, but I couldn't just let him go off. As he was walking over to her door, a policeman stopped and asked him a question. He responded and asked a return question. They seemed to be engaged in some kind of conversation. I couldn't hear the details. As long as he wasn't moving any farther away from me, I decided to keep my distance. The police officer kept him engaged for about five full minutes. Then he nodded and walked away with a glance at me.

I'm not certain, but I believe the police are just as aware of that 'distraction' strategy as we are. Everyone on that crime scene knew Michael's history and what we were all afraid of. I believe that police officer was reacting on instinct, as I was. Michael seemed to have forgotten about the bathroom and began wandering back to the curb. I trailed at my five to six foot distance and then approached closer.

"Darren needs to be with you tonight. You're his dad. He needs you."

"Darren is going to his aunt's house. That's what he wants to do. He needs to do what he wants."

Okay, there it was. We were involved in a sensible discussion. We were back to safe ground. I said nothing more and walked over to where Darren was sitting on the curb with his cousin. I squatted down directly in front of Darren and put my hands on each of his knees.

"Darren?" He raised his head halfway up. "Darren, you need to be with your dad tonight."

"I'm going to stay with my aunt, with Jimmy and my uncle, in Reading. That's where I used to stay."

"Darren, tonight you need to be with your dad. You should be together tonight. He needs you."

"All right."

I squeezed his knees and touched his head as I rose and walked back to where Michael was standing.

"Darren wants to be with you tonight."

He looked up and met my eyes for the first time. I held his glance for about five seconds, maybe ten, and then he lowered his head again. He stood there silently.

Then ...

"Where's Darren?"

"Over there by the curb."

He walked halfway across the grassy courtyard toward the curb.

"Darren?"

No movement. Then slowly Darren's slight figure unfolded from the curb and turned to face the voice of his father. They looked at each other for a moment and then each walked very slowly toward the other. Within five to six mutual paces they met, wrapped their arms around each other, and just stood there silently for a very long time. Then they shifted their grips to be side by side and walked away, out of the courtyard. I did not follow. I didn't feel worried.

I walked over to the crowd and began making my rounds again. The grandmother had been watching. She didn't say very much but gave me a halfhearted hug, or at least tried to. I spoke to Michael's wife and told her I thought that Darren might be staying with them tonight. She told me she thought that he was going with his aunt.

"Things change," I said. "Will it be a problem?"

"No. No problem. We still don't know where we're going to be. Probably just find a motel somewhere nearby. We're just not going back in there. Not ever."

"Can I make some calls and try to find you a room?"

"No, better wait for Michael. I don't want to do anything without Michael."

"Okay, fine."

That's kind of what TIP volunteers can do. We can find some lodging, make arrangements, but we can't transport anyone in our cars. Insurance liability and all that. But we can help out with logistical details. We can find a hotel room, a pet boarding facility, or an open pharmacy. We even contact the hazmat cleaning crew that comes to a crime scene after the police are done to clean up all the blood and body parts that may remain. In fact that is exactly what we would do later, before we left the scene. It can be a very expensive service, but your homeowners policy usually covers it. If not, we know of some companies that will actually work *gratis* (for free) in some situations. My partner and I discussed this service with the wife while Michael and Darren were off by themselves. I was able to explain our Resource Guide to her as well. She was the most in control and understood what I was saying. We gave her the coroner case number and other information. She agreed to let us take care of making the call to the clean-up company.

It was well after 10 PM when Michael and Darren came back around the corner of the courtyard, still with arms around each other.

Michael approached his wife and said, "Darren is staying with us tonight."

She nodded. That was that. I caught the grandmother's eye. What a team!

Michael's wife asked if we could retrieve some toiletries and other things from the house to take with them wherever they would end up. I told her I'd check and then walked over to the officer in charge. He told me it would be all right for them to enter the condo, but they had to stay on the first floor. They would not be allowed upstairs – nor would they want to go there. But if there was anything they needed, they could tell the officer inside, and he would fetch it if he could.

I told that to Michael's wife. She spoke with Michael, and the three of them walked slowly to the front door and entered. I followed.

Michael and Darren stretched out on the couch, nesting inward. Michael's wife spoke to the policeman at the foot of the stairs and described what she needed and where it was. He confirmed with me that nobody else would go upstairs and then went to get the needed items. It was quiet. He came down shortly with everything that had been asked for. Michael and Darren were curled up on the coach together. Darren had his eyes closed. Michael didn't. I think they were just catching their emotional breath. We all stayed where we were for a while.

Then Michael gently unwrapped himself from Darren, stood up, and announced to me that he had to go in the garage and get something from his truck. His chin seemed tilted up just a fraction. Courage? Defiance? Resolve? It was the loudest he had spoken.

My heart kind of froze. I felt I could not follow him into the garage. I knew I should, but I felt it insulting. I felt that we had made a connection. He made the statement to me, and I just didn't know what to do. Was he calling for help? For me to stop him? I didn't. I just walked up to the inside garage door he had gone through, which he closed behind him, and braced myself for the sound of a gunshot.

He came back in after a moment or three and kind of laughed. He looked at me and said, "Wanna see something funny?"

"Sure," I said.

He took me into the garage and showed me his truck. The front bumper was jammed against the wall.

"I guess I pulled in kinda hot!" He grinned a bit.

"Yeah, I guess so." I grinned back.

"I think I just want to back it off an inch and not permanently dent the wall."

He got into the truck, turned it on, and backed it up an inch. Then he turned it off and got out. We left the garage, and he told his wife what he had done. Back in the world.

My partner, Sarah, collected some additional clothes the policeman had missed and handed the bag to Michael's wife. The cleaners we had called finally arrived, and we walked out with the family. Sarah with the wife, Darren with his birth mother, who had been waiting outside the front door, and me with Michael.

I stopped on the porch with Michael and gently put my arm on his, came close and said, "Michael, at eleven this morning, I sat with a dad whose son had used a needle to end his life. It doesn't matter whether they choose a needle or a pistol or a bottle of pills. They're going to do what they're going to do. It's a terrible sickness, and it's not your gun that is to blame.

"I'm very sorry, but I can't do anything else for you tonight. You need to stick close to Darren. You need to listen to him. We're both dads, and I've learned more from listening to my son than I ever did from listening to my father. You need to be there for Darren. Don't leave him tonight."

Again our eyes locked. He said nothing.

We all paused at the curb. Sarah gave hugs to Darren, the wife, and the mother. Then Michael looked up and just reached out his hand to me, which I took. I guess it was a guy thing. He wasn't talking, but he had Darren in his sights.

I watched the three of them drive off in search of a hotel room and then said good night to the grandmother and the rest of the family while Sarah also said her good-byes. She checked to be sure the cleaner knew what to do with the key when he was done. It had been an eight-hour call on top of the four-hour call I'd had that morning. It was my busiest day yet. I don't expect to have another like it.

I don't know how much a recovering suicidal alcoholic whose father and son both committed suicide can endure. But he would get through this night. I believed he would. That was my job. I'm a TIP volunteer.

TIP is a national organization that serves hundreds of cities with over 1500 volunteers. In 1991, it won the prestigious Innovations Award cosponsored by the Ford Foundation and Harvard's John F. Kennedy School of Government. In 2000, Attorney General Janet Reno presented the Crime Victim Service Award to founder Wayne Fortin. Awards and national recognition reinforce the real rewards felt by the TIP volunteers every day, on every call. They just want to make a difference.

## Why do ordinary people do this extraordinary work?

What kind of people choose to put themselves in the middle of a human disaster? Certainly the police, fire, EMT, and ER staff all make that choice. It's a respected vocational path. But each of those professions has its own significant barriers to entry.

The overwhelming answer given by TIP volunteers to the *why* question is "To give back to the community." It's heard so often; 90 percent of my training class responded that way. But the words lose their meaning. What did this community give them that they feel some obligation to "give back"? Is this the real answer or the facile one?

In my limited experience, a TIP volunteer is most often a person who has suffered his or her own catastrophic personal loss: witnessing a stepfather murder a younger brother, coming home to find your son has committed suicide with your gun, watching helplessly by your wrecked car as life slips away from your wife while your son asks, "Daddy, what's happening?"

It wasn't just the death of a relative or close friend, but a horrific and traumatic death experience from which they need to heal and reconnect with the world. What many TIP volunteers express when questioned further is that being a TIP volunteer is part of their healing process. And healing doesn't just happen.

There's no end to the personal tragedies that occur every day in every town in the world. You can't relate to Darfur, Rwanda, Bosnia, or even the Holocaust. They are just words, pictures, stories told. You watch the *NewsHour*, see the pictures, and read the list of young soldiers killed in Iraq or Afghanistan. You might recognize a town or a uniform, a smile. But it's just for the moment. Then dinner is on the table.

Waking up to find your husband of fifty-four years lying in bed next to you, lifeless, will stay with you a lot longer than Katie Couric's nightly vignette. It has much more impact than the thousands of Iraqis or hundreds of thousands of Rwandans and Darfurians. When the coroner leaves after the body of your spouse has been 'transported', you are left alone in your home.

You're more alone than you've ever been in your life, and who is there to help you through these moments of disconnected insanity when your world has been vaporized?

Not the nice police officer who responded to your 911 call. Not the EMTs who did their best to restore a life that had been so entwined with your own. Not the coroner who was kind and gentle and patient with you in explaining how you could claim the body of your loved one after they had completed the autopsy. And yes, "Here is the coroner's case number for your reference. You'll need to give it to the mortuary to claim the body." The mortuary? The body? The deceased? My God, it was my husband, Bill, not *remains*. And then you are alone, sitting on the couch with a scrap of paper with a coroner's case number printed neatly, and that's all you have. That and the silence. And what do you do next?

What kind of person volunteers to stop his or her own life to be there for you, to help you get through those moments of unreality? That surreal feeling of emptiness, confusion, and anger. Floating above the room while your heart is nailed to the carpet, bleeding. Who is this TIP volunteer, and why is he there for you?

One answer is simple. Because there's nobody else in the system whose job it is to care for you. Sure, you should have family and friends, and that's what friends are for. But they're not there at that moment, that worst moment of all when you first realize the loss, the change that has altered your world forever. 9/11? Don't bother me. Katrina? A bad fairy tale. This was MY life that just ended. My life. What am I going to do now?

... marbles ...

Who am I living for now? Who do I make plans with, dinner for, complain to, hold?

The TIP volunteer has an enormous sense of compassion and has been rigorously trained to be dispassionately compassionate. The TIP volunteer understands the 'pit' you're in and is ready to get down there with you and gradually help you back to the reality of the world as it now exists. Why? Why do these people volunteer to inject themselves into the worst moments of somebody else's life?

Because they care? Yes, they do. Why? Because in expressing their compassion and their sincere caring, they often help themselves heal from their own horrific loss experiences. By genuinely caring for another human being, you somehow refill that emotional void in your own life. You fight back at the evil with just your own small effort of good. Little by little.

We understand the feeling of loss, but they also understand that we can't know how you truly feel in your uniquely horrific experience. It was your life. Your husband or child or parent with whom you had your own unique relationship filled with love and conflict and hope and resentments is gone. The TIP volunteer can't know what those details were or the individual regrets you have or hopes that have vanished. Just that they too had hopes lost, regrets forever unresolved, world imploded. The TIP volunteer knows that what you need right now and what they can offer is someone who genuinely cares about you and only you.

How does this help heal their own loss? It's hard for me to explain that to you here. Maybe a trained therapist can

try, but the clinical rationale is less important than what I
see: the genuine human warmth that comes through that fog
of overwhelming sadness, remorse, anger, confusion, and
frustration. Human compassion and caring can prevent the
'second injury' that occurs so often to the survivor. The second
injury that is so much akin to PTSD. The injury that results
from clumsy insensitive people who just want to say the right
thing, but don't know what it is. The neighbors that say,

"He's in a better place."

"I know how you feel."

"You'd better buck up and face reality. He's gone, and the
sooner you deal with it the better."

"You need to be strong for your kids."

"You need to contact the insurance company right away!"

"I have a friend who can help you with the financial side."

What you really need to do is to grieve for the most important
person in your world who is now gone. You need to feel the
anger and sadness and loss. You can blame yourself, your dead
wife, or God. You can feel whatever you want to feel without
filter. And you need somebody there who understands loss and
won't judge you. Somebody who can listen and feel your anguish
and validate it. Somebody who can support you and help you
make your own decisions about what to do now – but not *right*
now. Someone who can help you dial the phone to contact your
children or your sister or brother. Someone who can protect
you from the system that can be so callous. Someone who
understands that you don't really need that sister-in-law who

comes rushing in to embrace and cry with you for a moment and then gets down to meal planning and cleaning your house and making arrangements for you and insisting that you have to come stay with her because "You can't sleep here alone tonight" and just further removes you from the reality that is now your life.

Yes, there is a place for the helpful relative and close friend who can help you through these horrible times, but treating you like a helpless infant isn't always the best course of action.

TIP volunteers want to do good things because they understand that doing good things makes their world a little better, just a little. But that's all they can do. And that's enough for now. They aren't Albert Schweitzer or Mother Teresa, but we can help just one person survive just one personal disaster on this one day and stop the cycle of hurt.

That helps us believe that the world is a little bit better place and helps us heal and believe that our own personal loss is somehow counterbalanced just a bit. There's no protection from inevitable loss, but there is the opportunity to prevent the needless second injury.

Why do some people choose to be a TIP volunteer and others choose to strike back and attack when they are hurt? Some say that the healing we encounter is a reflection of the thought that, "Yes, I once suffered a horrendous loss, but that was years ago. Others are suffering right now. Just for today, this person is in worse shape than I am, so it makes me feel better by comparison. At least I'm not her."

Dr. Jayan Conily is the executive director of the Merrimac

Valley, Massachusetts chapter of TIP. Talking with her gives some clearer insights.

Just belonging to TIP is another way of healing. The essence of the insanity that takes us over during these crises is the disconnectedness to the world. That feeling of abandonment. "Nobody knows or could possibly feel the loss that I feel today. I am forever separated from society." But belonging to the TIP group helps us reconnect with people who understand the loneliness of the crowd. We rejoin society one small step at a time, and our monthly training meetings reaffirm our connectedness with this group of caring and compassionate people.

It may be that each of us in our quest to heal looks at each TIP call as another opportunity, an opportunity to return to that moment of our own when we were disconnected, scared, and helpless. We each climbed out of that ball of conflicting emotional confusion to try and reconnect with the daily reality of life. But we never really quite made it all the way. Our lives have been forever altered, and we just want things to be the way they were "before." By entering that moment in someone else's crisis, we may hope to revisit our own personal portal and try one more time to pick up the thread that had held our lives together. Each TIP call is just another chance to reconnect by going back to the source of our own departure.

Maybe not ...

And maybe the whole world is not such a terrible place after all. And maybe it's up to us, individually, to carve out the good little niche that we need to exist in.

Ask Wayne Fortin, the founder of TIP, and he'll tell you that some people say, "Because I can." They have a gift, and they feel responsible to use it. Many of them know they are good at doing this, and they like doing what they are good at.

Wayne will go on to tell you that others say they are "privileged" to be with people who welcome them into a very personal time in their lives. There is a positive aspect in being able to establish a relationship with people who are being "real" with all of their "stuff" stripped away.

"I want to prevent what happened to me from happening to others" is another quote Wayne will share. Learning about the human condition is another motivating factor.

Why does a person join TIP?

"To make a difference."

Just a little one. Better than doing nothing at all.

# Chinese food fantasy

## The frontiers of sexual reality

THE WORLD IS A SMILING FACE, usually female and often in bed clothes if you earn your daily bread delivering brown paper sacks of Chinese food around Brighton and Allston. After nearly forty months, there have been plenty of adventures, both pleasant and less than pleasant. Generally speaking, people receiving their dinner are smiling and grateful enough to tip a half a buck or so. Just enough for this mild-mannered reporter to support his small family.

You're probably curious about what sort of adventures could befall the humble Orient Expressman. Settle in. Here they come, and if you grow disinterested, we can digress to the tales of a former incarnation spent in the wonderful world of advertising. No, nothing like Putney Swope, Mason Reece, or Don Draper, but interesting enough if stories of multimillion-dollar budgets, ethnocentricity, and big business hold any intrigue for you.

What? Neither Chinese food nor big business beckons

seductively? Maybe you're a veteran of Kenberma Street on Nantasket Beach. A few nostalgic paragraphs about Paragon Park and the old Fun House with the enormous circular slide ought to do it. Or how about "Buck buck, how many fingers do I have up?"

I'm the Chinese food delivery man, former advertising executive, veteran of Kenberma Street and the US Army. Father of one with the dutiful wife at home doing freelance typing to supplement our drastically diminished household income. It's been interesting, if not profitable. Maybe we ought to begin in the summer of '74 at that now-famous dispensary of Oriental cuisine, Dragon Chef Restaurant.

Dum dee dum dum.

I was sitting behind the counter watching the Washington Street traffic go by. Sunday was slower than usual, not much to watch, which was a good enough excuse for getting caught in a conversation with a funny-looking fiftyish lady and her patient husband. They entered the front door together – he with a measured step, she with a slight limp – and made their way to the counter.

"Do you have that Mooshee chicken?"

"No. No Moo Chi," said Alan. Alan was the manager. He was about my age, twenty-seven, but a lot smarter. His wife, Christine, worked there too. Your value at Dragon Chef often hinged upon your ability to speak English. Alan spoke quite well and understood a lot more than he'd ever admit to. It always seemed easier for him that way. Inscrutable, you know?

"I just love that mooshee chicken, Irv. Ask again. Maybe he didn't understand."

"Do you have mooshee chicken?" said the smiling husband a bit louder.

"No. No Moo Chi,." repeated Alan.

"Oh, Irving."

"No mooshee chicken, dear. How about some egg foo young?"

"Oh, I don't know. Why don't you just handle it?" And with a deliberate neck swivel, she faced me.

"My name is Edith."

"Oh."

"My husband fixes air-cooled engines. His name is Irving."

"Oh." You gotta be kidding. Where is Allan Funt hiding?

"He works on Porsche engines and gets all dirty and greasy. You wouldn't know it to look at him. He's all cleaned up now. It's Sunday, you know."

She was right. I wouldn't have known it to look at him, and it was Sunday. No cameras. No Allan Funt.

Edith went on to detail several bodily malfunctions and malformations peculiar to her. It seemed that she was currently suffering from a loss of feeling in both the ring finger and pinky finger of her left hand. The trouble seemed to continue up her arm.

A twinkle entered her watery eyes as she raised her voice and quizzically quipped, "It seems to be growing shorter too."

Not missing a beat, she continued on into a litany of lower back problems that led to sleeping problems that led to ... um, personal problems.

Irv finished ordering around the time Edith started twinkling and had waited patiently for her to finish. I had the feeling he'd heard it all before. For some reason, Edith stopped and gleamed at Irving. I smiled, got up, and quickly walked back into the kitchen. That was about it. Four, maybe six minutes of entertainment on a slow Sunday. Well, no, not quite.

It was the following Tuesday night that I had a delivery to Newton Corner, an apartment building, up three flights, apartment 24 on the left at the head of the stairs. I knocked, the door opened against a chain, and eyes peeked out.

"Hello, Dragon Chef!"

The door closed, the chain rattled, and the door opened again on Edith in a housedress. Her left arm was definitely smaller and shorter than her right. One leg was bandaged, and her housecoat was as tacky as any I'd seen all month.

"Hi, Edith." Maybe a decent tip?

"Oh, hello there. You're the fellow from the Chinese restaurant." This was no surprise to either of us, but I recalled Edith's wavelength and chalked it up to a *different drummer* as I smiled.

"It's $12.75, please." Hoping for $14 and "Keep it."

"My leg's been bothering me all day. Would you like to look at it?"

I was ready to settle for $12.75 even. I reached for change for a twenty just to be prepared for a quick exit. I did not want to look at Edith's leg.

But there I was, looking in spite of myself. Edith got that

soggy twinkle, and she was off. With a remarkable stream of verbiage, she lowered her lumpy middle-aged butt into one kitchen chair and raised her foot onto another. She was actually removing the bandage from a very stubbly calf, refusing to allow me a word, grunt, or movement except to put down the dripping sack of egg foo young. The bandage came off, and I felt strange.

It wasn't the leg. It really wasn't. Sure it was nauseous looking, but I'd seen a lot worse at Brooke Army Medical Center at Fort Sam Houston back in '69. It wasn't even the odor. I think the strange feeling really came from a built-in alarm we all have. Something was wrong. Edith was less than attractive in any sense of the word, but I could sense that she had begun a successful seduction. There was no sign of her mechanic husband. In truth, I was no Dustin Hoffman, and no one ever mistook Edith for Anne Bancroft. Not even if I closed my eyes.

It just wouldn't be tasteful to detail the whole scene as it unfolded. To the best of my knowledge, Edith never ordered Chinese food again. She had spent at least twenty full minutes detailing diseases and afflictions that Sunday night. I can't honestly say I remember each malady, malaise, and malfunction, but there was one I'm sure she didn't verbalize. Edith left that one for my wife's gynecologist to explain.

# Kevin

*Tuesday 7/22/80*

*"31, get 115 Mokema ...*
*Waltham 31 ... Waltham 31 ...*
*Waltham three one ... 31 come in ...*
*Waltham 31 ... Waltham 31 ...*
*Twenty four get 115 Mokema ... Waltham 31 ...*
*come in 31 ..."*

KEVIN'S PROBABLY OUT of the cab dopin' up. Kevin's the only guy I ever met with the name 'Kevin' that I liked. It's only been three months driving, but there's something about night-drivers that breeds camaraderie. Lots of problems and no solutions, so you drive through the night laughing at the drunks, hoping for a run to Logan, smoking dope at the stand. Long hours spent on the same streets night after night build a relationship, almost a faceless one in the shadows of a driver's side window. Night drivers.

*"Thirty-one come in ... Waltham 31 ... Will someone run up to
Trapelo and Lex and see if that was one of our cabs that got
rolled over? ... Right, six seven, let me know. Waltham 31 come
in ... three one come in please."*

Kevin's got a cute wife and a new baby. He lives in the projects
and works days as a shipper on Calvary St. He's driving a cab
to try and save some money to buy a car. Little chance. Every
time he gets a hundred bucks together a gram of coke seems to
come around. He keeps threatening to go to school on the GI
Bill. He's twenty-five and could live nicely for those four years.
He's got some kind of disability pay plus an additional stipend if
he goes to school. He almost applied to UMass once.

*"Come in six seven. Right ... Is it the 31? ...
Right. I'll call Joe. He'll know what to do."*

Kevin was parked at the intersection of Lexington and Trapelo.
A nineteen-year old kid with two buddies aboard side-swiped
two cars on the way up Lexington by the Wal-Lex, got it up
to eighty miles per hour with the police siren screaming and
urging right behind them. The eighty miles per hour reduced to
zero as he slammed into the rear of Kevin's cab.

I was sitting in the Square and decided to swing over to the
hospital to see what was doing.

*"Waltham four seven get 5 Grant Place ... Right."*

5 Grant Place is the security guard at the hospital heading in
for his 11-7 shift. May as well pick up $1.20 on my way over.

## ... marbles ...

The heavyset Irishman slid into the front seat with his brown bag and thermos. I don't like people sitting in front, especially fat Irishmen with uniforms. They sweat a lot. I dropped him at the main entrance, then swung around to the Emergency, parked the cab and walked in like I knew what I was doing. I saw a nurse and asked if they had brought in Kevin Marquis, the cabbie.

They had.

I asked to see him.

She hesitated and asked if I was his employer.

"Sure."

His face was all cut up. The nurses had cleaned most of the blood away. His pupils were dilating back and forth. I never noticed he had very attractive blue eyes. He was awake.

Apparently when the car hit him, the windshield popped out and Kevin followed like a croquet ball. He landed on somebody's front lawn resulting in a helluva backache but no broken bones. He must have done a Superman across the lawn. It must have been a big yard. The cuts on his face were from his broken glasses and a bloody nose. He gave me a thumbs up and a weak handshake of sorts. We spoke a bit and I left. My bedside manner deserted me. He was alright. The cab had rolled three times and the gas tank was in the back seat, but what the hell. He had got in early that day and was driving my cab. So I sit writing this in a brand new air conditioned Impala. Thanks, Kev. All is not for naught.

•••

# ... marbles ...

*Dear Jerry,*

*Nana had a stroke last week. I guess mother told you. She's not putting up with it. Today she was walking down the hospital hallway. She's got use of one of her arms and one leg, but she can't hear out of her right ear and can't really talk. The side of her face sags. She has strength. When I went to kiss her cheek, she grabbed me and nearly sprained my back with the strength of her hug.*

*Beverly was there too. She hasn't changed much. The first thing she said was "Oh good, Bobby's here, Nana. I'll leave so you can talk to him." Nana grimaced. Then tried to smile. She's tough as nails. No shit. The doctor said it would be too dangerous to try and thin her blood to dissolve the clot. That means it either stays where it is or it moves. There's no winning on that deal. Nana is bullshit. She gets more bullshit when the nurses try their 'happy talk' routine. Beverly tries it too.*

*Rich Geller found this super lady about a year ago. She's about twenty-nine, real pretty, and manages the Statler Office Building. No shit. I went up to see her and she's a whole lot more than a rental agent. She's real clever, looks you in the eye when she speaks and has a great set of tits. She's got to be about the nicest thing that ever happened to Rich. He's been really dragging since his separation and divorce about three years ago. Heavy drugs, coke/Quaalude slingshot and all kinds of bad shit, but she really straightened him out. I've spent a couple of nights talking with her and was really overwhelmed.*

*I've never met a girl like that. She's even got a good name, Sigrid Holzman. She may or may not be Jewish. I don't know, but I'll find out tomorrow. I'm going to her funeral. She woke up this morning and jumped off the balcony of her luxury penthouse apartment.*

*I've gone back to seeing my shrink. I'm thinking about buying a booth in the Faneuil Hall Marketplace. They sell about $100,000 worth of Lucite key chains and things. I can get the money, about $50,000, from the SBA. I don't know. A shopkeeper's life sounds pretty boring to me. I've got nothing much to do though. I've kind of lost interest in looking for a job.*

*There's a pile of things I could tell you about, but I think I already told you already in my last letter. I hate to repeat myself. I just hate it. The weather for the past two-three weeks has been in the nineties each day. Kind of interesting. A real struggle to get through the days. And then there are the nights. One of these days I'm going to gather up the last few letters you wrote and try to fill your requests. It's just too hot to go poking around the house in Newton right now.*

*You may be interested to know that Dragon Chef is now serving Szechuan style food. Maybe some day they'll realize what we both already know; the home cooking they do in the back is much better than anything they serve in the front. It's only about 9:30 and there's nothing doing in Waltham. I'd put up, but I figure to wait around till 11 and try to say hello to Geller on my way home. Then again, he probably isn't much in the mood for company.*

# ... marbles ...

*Lisa has a Chinese girlfriend who lives down the street. She's very proud of the wooden 'kanji' name-plate you sent me. It's hanging on the front door as you instructed. She was so proud of it she wrote 'Daddy' on the upper right hand corner with a black felt tip. She wrote real small and didn't hurt it much.*

*You never said much about the Fleetwood Mac tapes. The critics didn't lavish the praise on it that they had for the previous albums. I felt it had real excellence that needed a lot of listening to appreciate. I think I also mentioned to you that it deserved playing on a decent sound system. So what do you think?*

## Wednesday 7/23/80

*Sigrid was not Jewish. No wonder I liked her. Today the rains have come. I find it cheery. Tomorrow I have two interesting appointments: One with the owner of the Quincy Marketplace stand, and second, with one of two publishers who have joined forces and are looking for a third to form a consortium of sorts. All things considered there should be some interesting discussion to spur me on through the weekend.*

*I have not reread the previous pages, though I'm sure the tone was moribund. Today is not, so why ruin things? Joany is getting married Saturday. Johnny had a party last Saturday night to celebrate. 'Free at last', huh? It was fun. He bought an island on Dudley Pond in Wayland and had about twenty-five people including numerous children for a cookout and stuff.*

*Lots of smiles.*

*I've got a few resumes to send out and lunch with a girl who's helping me put my condo guide together. I'd better get going. Might as well mail this and start again tonight.*

*Waltham 47 put'n up.*

*Love*
*Bobby*

# Remember *The Boatshu*

## The frontiers of a father/son relationship

JULY IN NANTASKET WAS GOOD. Getting up at 7 AM on a Saturday didn't matter as much because it was summer. I had my 'smart' best friend, Merrill, sleeping over for the weekend, and we were going out fishing with my father in his new seventeen-foot fiberglass speedboat with a big Evinrude seventy horsepower outboard mounted on a racing transom. Not really a boat designed for flounder fishing in Hull, but he got a good deal on it because nobody else in Nantasket was foolish enough to buy a lake boat for the ocean. Even the relative calm of the bay, where the chop never went much higher than two or three feet wasn't really what the boat designer had in mind. It was blue and white and sleek as hell from the bow to the swept-back windshield to the low, narrow stern. I couldn't wait to take it out myself during the week when he wasn't home to try to pick up chicks. I couldn't lose. Everyone loved to water-ski, and I had the equipment.

Merrill and I went to junior high together back in Newton. My folks had a summer house in Nantasket they had built in 1952. They had carved out an acre's worth of land from an existing apple orchard that sat just 100 feet from the shoreline of the bay. It was a helluva place for a kid to spend his summer. The bay was 100 feet up the street one way, the sandy ocean beach 200 yards the other way, Paragon Park just four miles west, and 100 teenage chicks in between.

Merrill and I had been grouped together in the 'smart' class at school to be guinea pigs in a new experimental math plan called Illinois Math. It was supposed to be a great new way to teach. I didn't pay much attention and found myself to be the only kid in the smart class who spent more time in detention than in the lunchroom. I guess I just tested well on all those standardized tests they give and consequently earned the label of 'underachiever' for most of my school years. 'Overtester' would have been more accurate.

Anyway, Merrill and I got to be really good friends. He was a bit wacky and joined me walking through the school halls with soda straws stuck up our nostrils. I got detention. He got warned to stay away from me. He paid no attention, and things worked out well. We both wore glasses. His had the Band-Aid in the middle of the bridge.

Although we were about the same size, he wasn't lucky enough to have the long, lean muscle mass genes that I had inherited. He was kind of soft looking, but strong underneath. He did not have much body hair at thirteen, while I definitely had good black arm hair and was already shaving every other week. Early on in our relationship, I had tried to give him the old 'tittie twister' in the locker room because he was so soft and fleshy looking. A short straight shot to my solar plexus dropped me to my knees. He was definitely strong. Mel actually ended up being quite a track star. Glad he didn't kick me.

It was the summer going into ninth grade. I was thirteen, horny, and obnoxious. I knew it all and let no one wonder. At five foot ten and 160 pounds, with a DA haircut and a Speedo, I was livin' large. Or in 1960 terms, groovy. This was going to be a pretty good day.

Merrill was at our summer house for a long weekend that found us making three circuits on the giant coaster at Paragon Park on Friday night. We spent some time in the fun house watching the girls get their dresses blown up over their heads by a secret air hose and then went on The Rotor over and over to watch the same girls slide down the walls of the spinning cylinder when the floor dropped out. They slid down about eight to twelve inches, but their dresses stayed right up there. It was a free panty inspection for anyone who cared to see.

Thirteen was a good age. Peyton Place had been published the year before, and I had permanent bookmarks on pages 70 and 123. Rodney Harrington was my new hero. Merrill and I reread those favorite passages before we went to bed in the back bedroom, and then before we knew it, we were woken by the Saturday morning sun with the added help of my father banging around in the basement as he collected the fishing gear.

I peeled off my underpants and took a quick shower to get

rid of the adolescent stink while Merrill was still rolling over a third time. I pulled on a pair of swim trunks and headed to the kitchen for some scrambled eggs and orange juice, courtesy of my omnipresent mom who always managed to time everything just right for my rush through breakfast.

"Good morning, Bobby. Where's Merrill? He has to eat something before you go out."

"He's comin'. Hey, Mel! Breakfast's ready!"

"You want some fresh tomato slices with your eggs? I just got them from the garden?"

"You got pepper?"

"Of course. Look at these slices. These are real beefsteak."

"Can I have some Frosted Flakes too?"

"Of course. Just get the box from the cupboard. Here's the milk. They said it might rain today. You better take some long sleeves with you. Make sure Merrill has long pants too."

"Yeah right, Mom."

Basement door opens to a ... "Are you ready yet? We have to get going. Where's your friend? The tide is coming in. Let's go."

My father had all three rods in his left hand and a large fishing tackle box in his right. He had on the usual uniform of untied sneakers, dirty bathing suit, and blue captain's hat. It was not the look of a dentist who spent sixty hours a week in a second-floor one-chair office on Brighton Avenue in Allston. He was 'The Doctor'. You'd best not forget it. This was his weekend deal. Boats and fishing.

In 1960, Nantasket Bay was as good as George's Bank.

We'd go out for an eight-hour day and come back with sixty to a hundred flounder. It was that simple. Drop your line with a double spreader. Let it hit bottom. Raise it up about six inches and wait. But not too long. The flounders bit like they were coming home. Most of the time you'd get about six pieces of bait from each sea worm, and more often than not, the fish would never swallow the bait, just the hook. You'd end up using the same slice of worm three or four times. A dozen and a half sea worms could bring home a hundred fish. It was fun. It made you feel like a winner. I had been fishing with my father since 1954, when I was about six years old. I knew how to bait a hook, remove the fish without bending the barb, and save whatever bait I could.

I drove the boat and got blamed whenever anything went wrong. I was a strong swimmer and had the job of swimming out to the mooring about fifty yards offshore, climbing in the boat, and bringing it over to the 'A' Street Pier for my father and whomever else was joining us to board. With this new fiberglass racer, there was a steering wheel and keys. Previous boats were just glorified wooden rowboats with an outboard that you started with a strong pull on the starter rope. This one was real classy, and I loved it. But I had to either hold the keys in my mouth when I swam out or put them in a pocket of the bathing suit. I had already learned the folly of that strategy. They just fell out when I was swimming. Luckily they had a bobbin attached and I was able to retrieve them followed by a good solid smack in the head from my father for being so stupid.

Merrill was just making it to the kitchen as my father was

walking out the front door.

"Hey, Skipper, have you got the sandwiches made?" my father yelled back to my mom.

"They're all ready, there in the bag. I made chicken and tuna fish. I didn't know what Merrill would eat. There are plums and peaches and pickles and potato chips. What kind of tonic do you want?"

But he was already out in the front yard looking out to the bay to be sure he could see our boat on the mooring. We were just one house down from the rocky beach. We could sit and watch the boat bob at the mooring at high tide, but he couldn't see the boat this morning because the tide was still low. He started walking up the street as he lit his first cigar of the day.

"Have you got root beer?" I asked

"Of course! And what do you want, Merrill?"

"How about some ginger ale?"

"Fine, we have plenty. I'll put in two cans. It will be a long day, and it gets hot. Here, Bobby. Take the cooler down and put some ice in it. I sliced up the tomatoes separately so they shouldn't make the sandwich soggy. I wrapped them in Saran Wrap, so be careful. The pickles are half-sour, and I threw in a sour tomato for Dad. There are some brownies for dessert and a few rugaluch I had left. I know how you love the rugaluch."

"Hurry up, Mel, Just eat a little. You don't get seasick, do you?"

"I don't know. I never went on a boat before."

"You never went on a boat? You gotta be kidding me! Can you swim?"

41

"Yeah, of course I can swim, but I just never went on anything except those paddleboats at Norumbega. I just never did. I think I may have been on a ferryboat once, but I don't remember."

"Are you sure this is going to be okay with your mother?" my mom chimed in.

"Yeah, sure. She lets me."

That was that. At least two out of the three of us could swim. It was always a joke around the neighborhood that my father couldn't swim a stroke. He spent more time on the water than anybody on the block and didn't even know how to float. My mother stopped nagging him after about three years and one or two aggravated backhands. His hands were big; they were dentist's hands, built for pulling teeth, cleaning fish, and swatting his kids and anyone else that got in the way.

Merrill took his plate to the sink, gaining my mother's everlasting admiration, and we were out the front door.

"Grab the cooler, will ya, Mel!"

I got to walk up to the bay carrying only a towel and a smile. May as well let Mel earn his keep.

I reached the railing where my father was waiting with all the gear. The bay was all rocks, and it was low tide. I hadn't worn sneakers. I never did. I would have to walk down the rocky beach about twenty or thirty yards, over the barnacles and mussels in my bare feet, before I got to the water's edge and then swim the fifteen or twenty yards out to the boat. The bottoms of my feet weren't entirely callused over yet. It was only mid-July, and it was definitely going to hurt.

"Here's the key. Don't lose it again!"

I took the key and tied the bobbin to the string in my bathing suit. It wasn't going anywhere. I dropped the keys inside the front of my suit, and it felt kind of funny. I started thinking about Rodney Harrington wading in the water on page 123. No time for that now. I had one foot over the railing as Merrill trudged up with the big cooler filled with food and drink.

"I'll be back in just a few minutes. Should I drive the boat up to the shore or meet you at 'A' Street?"

We were on 'D' street. The four blocks walking would be a real struggle for Merrill with the cooler, and my father didn't want to walk any more than he had to.

"Just pull it up in front here and be sure you don't scrape the bottom. Hurry up. The tide is coming in." said The Doctor.

I waded out to my waist and then started swimming. The bobbin in my pants was only a minor distraction. After ten or fifteen strokes, I was at the boat. Getting in with no ladder was another event. The low gunnels made it easy to get my arms over, but when I pulled my body over and in, there were always a few buckets of water that sloshed over the side. An inch of water on the bottom was no big deal. Merrill would get to bail it out once we were underway. I went aft and carefully lowered the big Evinrude, opened up the fuel cock, and pumped the rubber primer to get some fuel into the carburetor. Two steps to the front seat of the small boat and I was behind the wheel.

The keys came out of my pants. I untied them from my bathing suit string, put them in the ignition, turned the key clockwise, and the motor started right up. That was always nice to hear. I crawled up on the bow and released the mooring line while the motor idled and warmed up a bit. Back in my seat behind the wheel, I put it in forward and slowly eased it toward the shore. After ten yards, I reversed the engines so I wouldn't cruise right in on the rocks and get a whack across my head from The Doctor for screwing up the bottom of the boat. I had dug the engine prop into the mud too many times not to be careful.

My father waded out to catch the bow and swing it around.

"Merrill! Carry that stuff out to me and be careful not to drop anything!"

Mel took the cooler first and had little trouble carrying it out the ten or fifteen feet. It floated. My father swung it up to me, and I stowed it under the back bench seat by the gas tank. Merrill waded back and grabbed the tackle box in one hand and tried to get the three rods in the other, but he just couldn't manage. As they slid out of his grasp, he looked up, obviously feeling a little stupid and embarrassed, and just brought out the tackle box. He sloshed back to get the rods and the extra clothes my mother had sent along.

"Just throw them up to Bobby." Easy enough.

"Now swing your leg up over the side and get in."

I moved over to the other side of the boat to balance it so we wouldn't flip. Merrill struggled, as only a gangly thirteen-year-old can, but made it up and over. We both sat on the other side as my father grabbed hold and swung himself up. We were ready.

The Doctor took the driver's seat and headed over to the 'A'

Street Pier to buy bait. Merrill and I tagged along as he barked out his order.

"A dozen and a half. Make them fat."

He collected the brown cardboard bakery box filled with seaweed and eighteen fat sea worms that averaged about five to eight inches long, depending on whether they were stretching or contracting. I would get to teach Merrill how to bait his hook for the first time.

We silently trailed my father back to the boat and climbed in. Getting on board from the dock was considerably easier, although still not something to be taken lightly. A misstep would find you in the water or tip the boat so wildly that all the gear would slide to dockside, and then you had a real balance problem. Lake boats were really not for the ocean, no matter how sleek they looked.

The Doctor started the engine and told Merrill to put on his life preserver. He grabbed his own and put it alongside his seat. Merrill put his on. I released the dock ropes, and we turned for the middle of the bay. Father gunned the engine, raising the bow up high and dipping the stern, as all boats do. It was some kind of law of physics that I hadn't learned yet. We headed straight for Bumpkin's Island. I told Merrill about the old children's hospital that still stood in ruins on the island. It was a leftover project from World War II and abandoned soon after.

Decision time. Should we head for the Gut where the bay met the ocean and most of the fish could be found at the turn of the tide from low to high or should we go to the left of the island

45

near the shallow sand shoal that led into another branch of the bay? This was usually the best place when the tide turned from high to low and the fish began their return to the deep ocean.

The obvious spot was the Gut. Too obvious. By the time we got out at 8:30 AM there were already about fifteen boats anchored with two or three fishermen in each. You could even hear WBZ on their radios. We turned to port and went around the back of the island to find a half dozen more boats and then continued on to the sandy shoal. In a few minutes, we were there, and the tide was just too low. We could see the bottom. So we moved back toward the mainland a few hundred yards. My father cut the engine and told me to drop the anchor. This would have to do.

I let the anchor rope out about twenty feet to reach the bottom and then allowed another five or six feet for good measure. You didn't want to tie too tightly because the anchor would just pull out. I secured the line on the bow cleat and made my way to the back bench seat. My father was just about all baited and throwing his line over the side. I sat next to Mel with the bait box, opened the lid, stuck two fingers in, and pulled out an eight-inch beauty, black with reddish bristles and very lively.

Mel scrunched his face a little. I explained that you cut pieces about an inch to an inch and a half long and threaded the hook through the very center of the worm so no hook was showing. It was kind of like putting a sock on a foot. The best part was about the head. You put your thumbnail just behind the head of the worm and squeezed so that the mouth opened and those two huge fangs popped out. It was really scary looking. You plunged the hook right between the fangs and ran it down the throat. You never, Never had the mouth facing out. The flounder would never bite at that fanged mouth.

I baited my two hooks and then did it for Merrill just to show him how. We dropped our lines overboard and began the day. The fish were biting as usual. I hit first and brought one in within minutes. Then there was the ritual of getting the flounder off the hook and saving the piece of worm. I was good at it, despite the yelling of my father to be careful and not waste bait. My father unwrapped his second cigar of the morning, put on the radio to WHDH, and we were officially fishing.

We all pulled in our share as the sun rose higher and it got hotter. Merrill fit in well. He took off his life preserver pretty quickly and then his sneakers and then his shirt. It was hot.

By noon we had about thirty or forty nice wide flounder. Not a crab or skate in the bunch. It was a very good morning. We ate some fruit and then our lunch and just kept right on bringing them in. It was really exceptional. By 2 PM it had started to cloud over. By 3 PM we had close to a hundred fish and almost no bait. It was completely overcast but still very hot and humid. They were storm clouds. We weren't exactly in the middle of the ocean, so not to worry. We saw that big famous boat the *Randy Boatshu* go by. It was the fifty-five foot long cabin cruiser owned by the guy who owned Randy Boat Shoe Sneakers. Everybody knew the boat. It was the biggest in Hull Bay. They waved. We waved. Everybody waves when you're on a boat.

The fish did not stop biting. We were actually sitting a little lower in the water because of the weight of the hundred or so fish we were carrying, stored mostly under the back bench seat by the engine and gas. A rumble of thunder added an interesting little touch to the atmosphere. I smiled at Mel. I loved thunder and lightning. He didn't smile back.

"Maybe we should go in," he suggested.

"Naw, this is the best weather to fish in. When it rains, the flounder go crazy and really start biting."

The tide had just turned from high to heading back out to sea, and we were in perfect position. The fact that we were out of bait didn't seem to matter. I pulled a few stray pieces out of the mouths of some of the fish we had already caught. I just wrapped some seaweed around my hook. Anything worked.

The first few pitter pats of rain started coming down. They were large, warm droplets that made an audible splat as they landed. They felt wonderfully warm and soft.

"Waddaya say? Time to go in?" my father asked.

"No, it's getting good. We can get a hundred and fifty if we stay."

"Uh, I think we better go in. Isn't it dangerous to be in a boat when there's a storm?" Merrill offered.

"We oughta go. Just a few more minutes. We'll each catch just a few more," decided The Doctor.

Within a minute, the rain got steadier. Suddenly a bit of a chop in the water. There were two-foot swells. Now, two-foot swells are really nothing to worry about, except when your gunwales are only about eighteen inches above the waterline.

The first wave actually broke across the back of the transom, not over the side. It was a shocker. Suddenly we had about three inches of water in the bottom of the boat, and things were floating. My father saw the water.

"We're going. Now!"

" Pull up your lines and bail out that water!"

Another wave broke over the transom, and that wasn't good. The water was well over our ankles.

"BAIL goddamnit!" he yelled.

I dumped one of the holding pails full of fish in the bottom of the boat and used it to bail. It was a five-gallon plastic bucket, and one bucketful made a big difference. I got another bucketful out, and the biggest problem now was about thirty flounder all over the bottom of the boat.

"Clean up those damn fish. I'm going to pull up the anchor!" my father yelled.

Merrill just watched, not knowing what to do. The rain was warm, steady, and kind of nice. Then another wave broke over the transom and another right after. I grabbed the bucket and tried to bail. I barely got one bucketful over the side when another wave broke over the back. The motor was heavy, and the weight of the water pulled the rear of the boat lower. While my father was on the bow, it balanced off and no waves broke over the back. When he got back to the middle of the boat, we were just too low. One wave broke over the side and we were up to our knees in warm ocean water filled with dead flounder.

"BAIL" my father yelled. "I'm getting out of here!"

He turned the key to start the engine. It jumped to life, and the laws of physics dictated the bow of the boat rise and the stern dip. In this case, it dipped right under water, and the ocean flowed in.

"Shit. We're sinking!" my father shrieked.

We were swamped. Water rushed in. Dead fish floated around my eyes. Merrill grabbed his life preserver. My father turned, grabbed it out of his hands, and pushed him aside. Merrill grabbed my arm. The boat dropped deeper, and the bow popped up. There was an air pocket up front, and the tip of the boat just bobbed in the water as all our gear floated around us. Mel and I were close to the hull and grabbed on. My father had pushed off in panic and floated about five feet away, holding onto the life preserver he had grabbed from Merrill. He was wild-eyed with fright and spitting water. His cigar butt floated next to his face. His captain's hat was still on.

"Help me! Get me over to the boat! Come get me!"

I had some experience with the water and was a good swimmer. I had taken a junior life-saving class and remembered that drowning people tend to grab at you and take you down with them. The six-foot aluminum boat hook floated by, and I grabbed it.

I reached it out to my father and yelled, "Grab the hook. Grab the hook and I'll pull you in!"

"I can't! I can't let go of the life jacket!"

Time does slow down in these situations. I had the perfectly crystallized thought of forcefully jamming the boat hook into his cheek just between his eye and nose. Although they say the hand is quicker than the eye, the mind is quicker than both. That option clicked clearly in my mind, but my arm never wavered an inch. I gently extended the end of the boat hook.

"You don't have to. Just open your hand, and I'll get the end in your palm."

He did, and I did.

I pulled him the few feet to the bobbing bow. He grabbed on too. We floated there for a minute, realizing what had happened. Dead fish still floated all around us, along with seat cushions and other gear. Some of the fish started to sink.

"They win after all," I thought.

The waves started to break in our faces. That was no fun, especially for Mel and my father.

"Let's get on the other side of the hull. Then the boat will break the waves for us," I said.

We walked our hands around the bit of bow that still bobbed in the waves until we were all on the other side. Being leeward was a big difference. It was okay now. It was okay. The bow seemed as if it would bob forever. It hadn't gotten any lower. It was fiberglass, and the air pocket that kept it afloat was pretty secure. We just sat and bobbed in the water for three to four minutes, making sure we had good handholds on the bobbing bow. The rain kept up. The thunder rolled in. A few streaks of lightning added to the fun. Merrill whimpered just a bit. This was not a great first boating experience.

I didn't like just sitting there. No one was going to come

get us. All the sensible fishermen had already gone in. I saw the *Randy Boatshu* about 250 yards away. It was turning and heading back to the pier. They couldn't see us; we were barely visible amid the two- and three-foot swells.

"I'm going to swim over to the *Boatshu* and get their attention. No one will ever see us just sitting here."

"Can you make it? Where is it? I can't see." my father said.

I pointed.

"Can you make it that far?"

"Yeah, sure I can." I really thought I could. I'd always been a strong swimmer, so a few hundred yards was not going to be a question.

"You okay, Mel?"

"Yeah, I think so. But hurry. Okay?"

"Yeah. I won't be messin' around. Have you got a good hold on the boat?"

"Yeah, just keep your father away from me."

"Don't worry. He won't move. He's scared to death."

I stroked out into the bay. The first thing I realized was that swimming in a three-foot swell was a lot different than swimming in the calm. I pulled about twenty strong strokes and looked back to see that I had gone barely ten yards. This wasn't going to be as easy as I thought. No time to worry about it. Let's get strokin'!

I swam about another forty strokes and was getting a little winded. I stopped for a minute to get my bearings and catch my breath. I could see the *Boatshu* dead ahead. It didn't seem at all closer. I looked back and saw the white hull bobbing in the waves. I was only about twenty-five yards from where I had started. How was I going to make another two hundred? And what way was the *Boatshu* heading? If it ever got going fast, I would be lost. No time to rest. I pulled forward and just put my head in the water and stroked. I went another twenty yards and had to rest. The *Boatshu* seemed no closer.

I couldn't see the bobbing bow anymore. This was not a good situation. My arms ached. I backstroked for a while in the right direction just to get some rest. Let my legs do more of the work. I caught a glimpse of the bow, still bobbing.

Back over on my stomach, and more strong stroking. Well, it was strong for the first three strokes. Then my arms started getting heavy. Maybe the sidestroke would be better? Yes, it was better. It was easy. Stretch your arms and scissor- kick. Stretch and kick. I could do this all day. But I couldn't see where I was going as well. I rolled over on my front and went back to the crawl, but not for very long. I looked up and the *Boatshu* just didn't seem any closer at all. I started to notice the rain coming down heavier. May as well try the breaststroke. I just had to stay afloat. I'd get there somehow. I just had to stay afloat.

My arms were just dead. My legs were still strong. Time to float a bit. Get some rest. Breathe deep, in through my nose out through my mouth, in through my nose – but the rain was coming down hard and into my mouth. I just had to get to the *Boatshu*. Back to the sidestroke. Reach and scissor, reach and scissor, reach, and there was a big wave and a noise and a little boat pulled up alongside me. It was a nice tan wooden boat with a green bow stripe, and a pretty lady in a two-piece bathing suit leaning over the side, reaching for me and yelling. I couldn't really hear. But she had a wonderful cleavage.

"I've got to get to the *Boatshu!*" I yelled. I was not really all there.

"Get in. Get in. We'll take you!" she yelled. She was definitely pretty. She had long black curly wet hair and green eyes. She had a wonderful cleavage.

I realized I was saved just about a minute before I realized I needed saving. I took another minute. Then I just wanted to get in the boat. I held on to the side and tried to pull myself up. I saw a man with a beard at the wheel looking back and yelling something to the lady. The boat was small, and I was starting to tip it with my struggles. The lady went over to the other side of the boat. I tried again to pull myself up, but the side of the boat was now much higher in the water and my arms wouldn't work. I just held on. That was fine with me. I was safe, but we had to get back for Mel and my father.

I couldn't move my arms. They started to cramp into position over the gunwales. Then the guy with the beard was back with me and leaned over. He grabbed the back of my bathing suit with one strong hand and pulled my ass over the side. A wave came in with me as the side dipped. But this was an ocean boat, and it was no real problem.

I lay on the small deck and said, "My father. My father and my friend. We swamped. Back there. We need to get them."

"Where?" she asked, looking around.

I sat up and could barely see over the side. I didn't see them. I looked all around and saw the *Boatshu* still moving slowly and still more than a hundred yards away. I looked back in the opposite direction to find my father and Mel. I saw nothing but rain and waves.

"Back there. Somewhere. Just drive over there and we'll see them." I hoped.

He turned the bow in the direction I had pointed and hit the throttle of a pretty powerful inboard that I felt thrumming under me. We moved forward. I looked and looked and looked. She was looking too. He was steering and looking. Then I saw a patch of white. Then I saw it again.

"There. There they are." Just about fifty yards away sat the bobbing bow with Mel and my father still hanging on. The man with the beard pulled up alongside and pulled Merrill up first.

"I can't swim. I can't swim!" my father yelled.

"Give me your hand!" the man yelled.

"I can't. I can't let go!"

"You have to. Just reach over to me!"

"I can't let go! I'll drown! I can't swim."

I didn't think much. I just jumped over the side and back into the water. Big mistake. I was bone weary and could barely keep afloat. I held on to the bow next to my father and told him it was okay. We were saved. He just had to get in the boat.

"I can't! I can't let go. I'll sink ...," he trailed off into a whimper.

"Put your hand on my shoulder. I'll hold you up."

He thought for a second and then grabbed my shoulder and pushed me right down under the water. I still had hold of the bow and pulled myself up again. This wasn't working.

"Grab my arm Grab my arm!" the bearded man yelled.

"Grab his arm!"" I gasped. "I've got you."

My father must have reached over and grabbed. I was underwater again. I came back up to see him draped over the side of their boat, his dentist's ass in the air. Then the man pulled him the rest of the way. He was in. I was happy. I was calm. I was tired. I just wanted to rest. I floated there for a bit with my eyes closed, just resting. The pretty lady was shouting to me. I didn't care much. I was warm. I was floating. It was very quiet except for her shouts.

Then I remembered how pretty she was and opened my eyes. She was waving and screaming at me to get in. The bearded man was back behind the wheel, trying to get closer because I had drifted away a bit. Then they were alongside. Then I was in the boat. My father was seated along the side. Merrill was up front in the mini-cabin. I crawled forward to see how he was doing.

"Nice tits, huh!"

"You're an asshole, ya know. A real asshole."

"Yeah, but she does have nice tits."

"Go fuck yourself."

Both of our eyes were wet – mostly from the rain and the ocean, but not entirely.

Hanging there on the crossbeam of the bow was a crucifix.

Merrill and I smiled at each other. Maybe it was time to learn what the *Goyim* were all about. They certainly were in the right place today.

The bearded man circled around the white fiberglass bobbing bow. My father was yelling for him to tie a rope to it and tow it in. The bearded man wasn't having any of that garbage. There was a major storm happening. His boat wasn't that much bigger than ours, and ours was swamped. We headed in to the 'A' Street Pier.

On the way, my whole body cramped up in one big convulsion. It was like a steel trap had sprung, and every muscle was contracted. It hurt. Then it went away, then I slept for a minute. Then I was awake with the pretty lady looking at me real closely. We tied up to the pier. Merrill and my father got off. I started to and fell down. The bearded man helped me up and onto the pier.

"Hey, what's your name?" I asked. "I don't even know your name."

He told me.

"Can you write it down for me, and your phone number too. I really want to thank you, and I'll never remember."

He said sure and gave me a scrap of paper with some scribbling on it. I took it and shook his hand, her hand, and then started to walk down the pier toward the shore. It was still raining and getting even darker. The thunder rolled over and over, and the lightning flashed, and I was suddenly sitting on the pier to rest. The little piece of paper blew away on the wind, and that was all I remembered until I heard my father yelling at the guy at the pier bait shop to go out and pick up his boat. Merrill was sitting next to me.

My mother appeared and was all crying and hugging and everything. No big deal. We were all okay. Merrill had lost his glasses. My father promised to pay for them and never did. He claimed they were already broken anyway. The *Randy Boatshu* ended up towing our swamped boat in the next day. The motor was totaled. The boat itself was fine, but no one else in Nantasket Bay was foolish enough to want to buy it.

We got a bigger wooden boat the next summer. But that blue and white fiberglass model was sure fast, and great for picking up chicks. I never saw the man with the beard or the pretty lady again.

# Frank

## Frontiers of mortality converge with morality

"FRANK!"

Thump.

Disfigured bloody face with gaping mouth on my windshield? Broken glasses askew?

Gone.

"FRANK!"

Thump, thump.

Huh? Shit!

"Fraaaank!"

What the fuck? Oh, shit. I hit somebody. Somebody named Frank?

The screams of "'Frank! Frank!" continue. Was it an echo? No. Somebody was hysterical. I think I hit somebody. I know I hit somebody. Stop!

Left foot clutch. Right foot brake ... hard.Stop.

Right hand bumps the stick back from third into neutral.

Oh, Shit. I hit somebody. That lady has to stop screaming.

There was a red smear on my windshield. Just a little. But I saw his face. Well, his mouth anyway. His mouth was open. It was like he was sucking on my windshield. But he wasn't. He must have rolled off the hood. To the left. Yeah, he rolled off to the left. I have to get out.

The TR4-A was a great little car. Real low. Not real easy to get out of, but at twenty-one I was still pretty limber, sprung out easily and looked behind me. There was a body in the road. It wasn't moving. It was dark, about 9 PM, and I couldn't see very well. But he, Frank, I guess, wasn't moving.

I ran over to him. The lady screaming "Frank!" had stopped screaming and ran over too. I got there first.

"Call an ambulance!" she screamed. "Call the police!"

I didn't say anything. I just looked at the body lying face down. Not moving.

*Shit. I hit somebody.*

I didn't touch the body. I didn't get any closer than kneeling over him and wondering, *What?*

The lady started screaming again. Neighbors came out. Porch lights came on.

The police arrived. An officer called me aside and asked what had happened. We sat in my car. My '67 BRG Triumph TR4-A. I loved that car. It had been a college graduation present. I answered the officer's questions.

"I saw a guy in the road. Walking across the road. Left to right. I swerved left to avoid him. I guess he must have stopped

60

or backed up because I didn't avoid him. He was wearing all dark clothing. Dark pants, an old suit jacket, dark shoes. Just didn't see him until it was too late."

That face on my windshield, the open terrified eyes, the mouth and lips sucking on my windshield. I didn't tell him that part.

"Well, he is alive and on the way to the South Shore hospital," the cop said. He was nice. He wasn't just a "cop." He was nice. He seemed to feel badly for me.

"Have you been drinking?"

"No. No. I just got off work. I work in Quincy. I'm kind of an assistant manager at a deli. I cook a little. I take care of the cash register. I got off at 8:30. Long day. I wasn't drinking. Just tired. Twelve-hour day. Twelve and a half, actually. I'm on my way home. I mean, I was on my way home. Now this."

"Yeah. Well, I don't smell anything on your breath. Would you mind stepping outside and walking around for me?"

"Sure. Sure. But I'm tired, really tired. I don't know how I'll do, but I wasn't drinking. You can test me. I wasn't drinking."

I walked around a little for him and touched my nose and I don't remember what else. I saw a whole bunch of police cars around. I saw an ambulance. Lots of flashing lights. It felt sad, just very sad. Tired and sad. Two officers were wheeling a unicycle kind of thing down the road, measuring something or other.

"What are they doing?" I asked the nice officer who seemed to be my friend.

"They're measuring your skid marks," he said

Skid marks? What skid marks. I didn't skid. I just stopped. I didn't skid. I was in control. I am in control. I'm just tired. Tired and sad.

"Come back into the car with me," my friend said.

So I did. I ducked down into the driver's seat of my beautiful BRG Triumph TR4-A. I noticed that there was a little dent on the bonnet. The bonnet is what they call the hood of British cars. BRG means British Racing Green. I had a little dent in my bonnet, and there was still a red smear on the windshield. Not very much really. The windshield didn't break or anything. It really wasn't so bad. Was it?

"The man you hit is alive and on his way to the hospital. I don't detect any alcoholic influence. The length of the skid marks indicates that you weren't going more than thirty or thirty-five miles an hour. But you did hit a man. If he were dead, I would have to arrest you. If you were drinking, I would have to arrest you. But he's alive, and I don't detect any alcohol. I suggest you continue on your way home and stay there for the night. We'll be in touch with you. I'm sorry this happened."

Sorry? Yeah, sorry.

"Thank you," I said. "Thanks a lot. I'm sorry, really sorry. I'm tired. I need to get home."

"Drive safely," he said.

"Yeah. Very safely."

I turned the key, started the engine, put my left foot on the clutch, and shifted into first. My hand was shaking. My left foot felt weak and trembling. I slowly accelerated forward and down the dark road, hoping that it was a dream, knowing it wasn't.

But hoping, hoping I don't know for what. Just hoping.

Ten days later, Frank Lefreniere died. I had already called a lawyer. The older brother of my college roommate had just graduated law school, and he was very happy to get the business. The short story was that all the evidence the police could gather showed that Frank Lefreniere, seventy-two years old, was dead as a result of being hit by my British Racing Green Triumph. He apparently died from some kind of head trauma. Both his tibias had been broken by impact with my bumper. He had multiple skull fractures from the impact with my windshield and then the road. He had lingered for ten days, but then lingered no more.

I would automatically lose my license for six months. That was statutory in any vehicular fatality. The reports did not indicate that I was driving recklessly, under the influence, or with any negligence. I just killed the guy. He wasn't watching where he was going when he crossed the dark street at night and zigged when I zigged instead of zagging. I killed him, but I was not to blame.

I don't think the lady who shouted "Frank!" felt the same way. I was not criminally responsible. It was just an accident. But they sued anyway. My car insurance covered me for $50K. They wanted $500K. After two years of legal bullshit, they settled for the $50K from the insurance and another $10K I had managed to save up over the time.

But Frank was dead. I never thought too much about him after that. I tried to get close to the idea of having killed somebody, but it never took. I was kind of sorry, but with no real remorse. You know what I mean? No crying jags. No overwhelming guilt.

## ... marbles ...

Shit happens, and it happened to Frank Lefreniere. He should have zagged. I was a lot more concerned with going to Viet Nam and having it happen to me.

Sorry, Frank. Life goes on ... without you.

# Mother

THREE YEARS BEFORE MY MOTHER starved to death in a nursing home in Needham, Massachusetts, my older brother decided that he would not forgive her for staying married to our father. Further, he decided not to speak to her again. She was seventy-eight years old at the time of his decision. He was fifty-five.

It was relatively easy for him. He had been living in Kyoto and then Osaka for the previous twelve years. What with the thirteen-hour time difference and all, ending communication was little challenge. He succeeded in his resolve.

My mother never understood why he had abandoned her. He never actually bothered to tell her, but I tried.

At the time she had been undergoing radiation therapy for brain cancer. Her equilibrium was gone, most of her sight had been burned out of her brain. But her cognitive skills had been left unimpaired. Still, she didn't seem to understand why, after fifty-five years, he would do such a thing.

I learned after her funeral that she had actually tried to accommodate my brother's wishes just six months after her marriage to my father, The Dentist. She felt she'd had enough – actually, more than enough – packed her bag and went home to her parents' house just a half mile away. They allowed her to stay the night and then another, but then insisted she go back to her husband. Divorce was a *shander*. This was 1939, and divorce was not an option for a nice Jewish girl of twenty-two. Not even for a college graduate with a law degree from Portia Law School. She had to go back. This was her life now.

She had tried to satisfy my brother before she even knew him. That effort continued all her life, always trying to satisfy him, never knowing him. I don't think he was aware of that, and I'm not sure it would have mattered. His brain was more damaged than hers.

Her death was a drawn-out ordeal. It seems as though it may have begun the day she was born, but the climax was a seventeen-day fast due to a series of strokes that first took her sight, then her speech, and then her swallow reflex. Or that's what the nursing home caregiver had said. I wasn't sure I entirely believed that.

Given the circumstances, I would have given up eating as well. My uncle used the same tactic four years later in similar circumstances. When you're done, you're done. No point in feeding the beast any longer. But my father had insisted that they continue to bring her meals each day. After all, he was paying, or actually Medicare was paying. Somebody else was paying, and he wasn't missing a free meal. He actually was quite confrontational about it with the nursing home director.

## ... marbles ...

He was a lucky kind of guy with great timing, my father. It was just two weeks before my mother's final stroke that the nursing home had decided to stop providing meals for him. He would come every day at lunchtime to visit. Every day, at exactly 11:30 AM, he showed up. The Jamaican nurses would cluck and chuckle and make overt gestures of checking their watches as he marched in. At first, they thought it was touching that he visited every day and offered him an extra tray of whatever it was they were serving that day. Then, my father, being who he was, demanded a menu so he could select what he would get the next day. The nurses didn't mind and found it something to laugh about. After about a year, the nursing home director somehow got wind of it and decided it was not in his budget.

That didn't bother my father too much. Being an industrious and creative sort, he just began eating my mother's lunch. She was already half blind and couldn't see what she was given. He told her she needed to go on a diet and shared a spoonful or two before he finished the rest. He'd usually give her a bit of the soup and laugh because it tasted watered-down anyway.

"May as well give it to her. She doesn't know the difference," he always said.

Then at the end, when she'd had her series of strokes and couldn't eat at all, it was the last straw for him. He made a scene, intimidated all the orderlies and attendants, and was finally escorted to the director's office where he could still be heard shouting behind the closed door. He got his free lunches for the almost eighteen months she lay dying. I'm not sure what he did for lunches after that. I know I didn't provide them.

I sat with my mother holding her frail right hand every minute of those last eight hours. She was comatose and breathing very heavily, panting actually. It was clear she was dying, and I felt it wrong to let her die alone. I'm not sure what comfort I may have been at the time. I know I wasn't much comfort to her when she was alive.

Her enduring words to me were, "Bobby, dear, I may not like you, but I must love you. I'm your mother."

And that may have been true, certainly the first half. Who knew what her definition of love was, what with a son who abandoned her in her final three years of life, parents who had emotionally abandoned her when she was twenty-two, and a husband whom she had wished all her life would abandon her. But he had kept coming home for supper, night after night after night, for fifty-seven years. Now that was love. At least, that was what she knew of it, so maybe she did love me after all.

Sitting there for eight hours gave me time to think, forced me to think actually. I kind of feel that I had a Vulcan Mind-Meld with my dying mother. At least at the very end, I'm sure we were both thinking the exact same thought: "Just stop breathing already."

I must say that I had loved her, though I didn't really know it, not then. Not at just forty-nine years of age. It took several more years for me to really learn what love is (with apologies to the group *Foreigner*).

It took the birth of Emma, my granddaughter.

# Dedicated to Emma

## Open adoption

*Dad,*

*I know how you hate when I beat around the bush, so I'll just tell you that Holly is pregnant. I'm not going to San Diego State as planned. I'm going to stay around here until the baby is born and go to Framingham State. It should only be a minor inconvenience for a few months and delay my plans just a little.*

*Dano*

I WAS SITTING IN MY HOTEL ROOM at the Best Western-Miramar in San Diego, reading this letter from my young son and thinking that we were dealing with something more than a 'minor inconvenience'. At seventeen, Dano really didn't know that. He would learn.

Daniel had recently discovered his first real girlfriend. Holly had long auburn hair, a smile like a Madonna, and a nose ring.

She was a regular visitor to our home in Holliston and, we later found out, an occasional overnight guest. It was on my next business trip that I received Dan's letter.

I came home to learn that Holly was against abortion but that they were not going to base a marriage on a careless act. They felt a great deal of love for each other but didn't think a high school marriage was a great idea. They would give the baby up for adoption. Dan, Holly, my wife, Carol, and I all hugged.

The adoption agency suggested Holly and Dan consider an *open adoption*, in which the adoptive parents are chosen by the birth parents. They would all get a chance to meet before the birth. After the baby is born, there could be some level of ongoing contact. There would be no secrecy. Still, Carol and I had eight months of serious questions and judgments ahead.

Dan and Holly received folders from five prospective adoptive couples that included homemade brochures telling us who they were and why they would be a good choice. Carol and I selected a couple we liked. Dan and Holly independently chose the same couple. They liked their musical backgrounds. Carol and I liked the fact that they seemed unpretentious.

The next step was a meeting. Dan and Holly were nervous but came home pleased. There would be more meetings. Next, they went out for dinner, to a club where they listened to jazz and got to know one another better. The feelings of comfort grew. Visits continued.

I decided I wanted to meet these people and was about to call when the phone rang. It was Jim, the prospective father, calling to say hello. He had heard from Dan that I wished to meet and was calling to see how that might work.

Carol said she was too nervous to go, but at the last minute she changed her mind. We met at a bagel place on Route 9 in Framingham. They were there waiting.

Jim and Dale shared pictures of their family, their home, and their dog. They were in their early forties and lived in a suburb of Boston. They had met at an audition and traveled to Paris together after they graduated from college. After an hour of preliminaries, we relaxed. We talked some more and cried a bit.

Three hours later, we hugged. There were a few more tears. I couldn't believe the warm feeling inside. For the first time, I had begun to see some good in all this. These two folks were about to get the best gift life can offer. They seemed like deserving, patient people.

Leading up to this meeting, I'd had the overriding thought that you don't give away your children. I wouldn't let the idea of keeping my grandchild escape. There was little I could do. It was Holly's decision along with Daniel's advice and consent. It was my grandchild, but I was a bystander.

Holly's mother, Diane, turned out to be a wonderful partner in this struggle. She was certainly devastated. She was a single parent raising two daughters on her own. But she is a caring person who has become a good friend and member of our extended family. Rather than take an angry, adversarial position, she chose to see us all as allies struggling for the same goal. It was hard on Diane, having Holly decide to live with us, but she saw no benefit in creating more conflict.

After meeting with Jim and Dale, I felt as though the door had opened. I saw there was another side to this event, a genuinely good and wonderful side. I began to believe, and I tried almost desperately to nurture that belief.

## Friday, November 3, 1995

Emma was born at Framingham Union Hospital. We had thirty-six hours to get to know her.

On Sunday, Jim and Dale arrived. I watched Dale fuss over her diaper with Jim looking on in a confused state of euphoria. Jim and I embraced in a long, tearful bear hug. I kissed his wet cheek, gripped his outstretched hand, wished them both all my love, and left quickly.

Holly and Dan had signed seven-day foster parent papers so Jim and Dale could take Emma home. They were to sign the permanent ones after that.

After the week was up, we received pictures from Jim and Dale with a lovely update note. Holly and Dan signed another set of temporary papers. Holly was not ready for the permanent documents. She had some things to sort out – things she wanted to know, questions, doubts, a lot of pain. Between the physical postpartum issues and her milk coming in, there was measurable physical discomfort. The emotional side defied description. She was struggling mightily. She'd had her seventeenth birthday in August. She was so much older now.

Another appointment was made to sign the final papers. It was for the Wednesday before Thanksgiving. Holly canceled it.

I was worried. This was not good for anyone. I pressed Daniel to encourage her to do it. He would not be moved. All in good time. He knew what I was saying. He understood. He also understood Holly, and of course he had feelings too. Thanksgiving came and went.

That Friday, at 1 PM, they drove to the agency and signed the papers. They came back home and went right to their room. It was numbing.

The weekend days passed slowly. Few words. Many silent hugs. Hands were held constantly, quietly. The weekend ended. Monday began. It's been one day at a time since.

## January 14, 1996

Now we deal with the reality of what *open adoption* means. We're learning. We've received two more photo packets from Jim and Dale: Emma's first bath, first doctor's visit, and other things.

Carol and I are confused. How is this going to work? Don't Jim and Dale want a little distance? How generous and kind of them. What gear do we put our emotions in? Will this continue? At what pace? Can I be a part of Emma's life even at a distance? I don't know.

Carol cries a bit out of frustration. I'm just filled with wonder. Carol thinks the letters should stop. I'm waiting and learning. Dan and Holly seem fine with it. I saw Holly reading a book on open adoption. There are things to be learned. I think a seventeen-year-old girl with the smile of a Madonna is going to teach me. She lost the nose ring last October.

*Dear Jim and Dale,*

*Planted in the sitting room of the Colonial Inn on a rainy Saturday afternoon was not what I would have envisioned as the setting for our first visit with Emma and her parents. What seems consistent is that my visions of what will happen are remarkably inaccurate, yet what actually does happen is quite wonderful.*

*Non-planning and no expectations are two of the ingredients I choose to bring to our relationship with you and Emma. I feel secure in the knowledge that Holly and Dan made the right decision, and they know that. Most important is that they are both happy with it and continue to grow more comfortable as the days pass. Second most important is that Emma is happy. Having seen her for about ninety minutes, I am left only with the impression of happiness, contentment, good health, and a very alert mind that seems to be acutely aware of her surroundings and not at all threatened by them. Third on my list are the two of you. I think you're happy too. Sorry for placing you third, but I'll bet you understand.*

*In talking with Jim, I was concerned to hear what seemed to be a level of anxiety. My guess was that it stemmed from many things. One was wondering what was best for Emma. Are we creating a potentially confusing emotional environment for* her? Another diminishing concern was over Dan and Holly's attitude in regard to the situation. Third, though unspoken, must be the everyday anxiety new parents have over their child and their role as parents. Fourth might be a fear of others' trying to enforce their will, their presence, and their values on you and Emma.

Dan and Holly's attitude has been healthy. They've dealt with the pain. Holly, in particular. They have learned a basic lesson of life. We are faced with difficult decisions and must do what we believe is best. Most often it isn't the rightness or wrongness of the decision, but rather what we make of the results that determines our happiness. They are making the best of the results and enjoying unexpected happiness. That feeling grows daily.

Please know that we welcome any opportunity to share, but will show the same sensitivity to the situation that you both already exhibit. We are concerned about the two of you and your comfort. It's a direct determinant for the happiness of your daughter. If you are looking for some additional family, allow us to submit our resumes. If you choose to go part-time to begin with, that's great. If you choose to wait and see, that's fine too. If you choose to insulate your private lives, that's part of the deal that we accept with no strings at all.

*xx*

oo

*bb*

## February 26, 2003

Emma is seven years old. Holly and Daniel are young independent adults who have reconciled some ambivalence between them and become friends again, remaining connected through Emma. We have grown to know Jim and Dale as people, not just the parents of our granddaughter. We have met their families and enjoyed every minute of the many get-togethers that are far more frequent than the gatherings of our own pre-Emma family. It's like having in-laws without the angst.

Emma is the typical seven-year-old, with a funny intuitive innocence. She came home from school one day after discussing brothers and sisters with her classmates and asked Dale to call Holly and Dan. It seems the other kids had a brother or sister, and she wanted one too.

"Please ask Holly and Dano to make me a sister," was her request. Nothing more. Just a knowing grin.

Her open adoption had made her a minor celebrity at school. Of course, there are the typical stories that come from any seven-year-old with missing teeth.

"I'm having trouble saying my Ws and can't pronounce 'world' very good, so I just say 'earf' instead."

When Emma asked whether Dan could fly in from Tempe, Arizona, to escort her and her dad to the father-daughter dance at school, our jaws dropped. After a moment's thought by all, Dan bought his ticket from America West, and Emma was the only girl in the second grade who had two dates for the dance.

She made introductions to all. The trio had a great time.

Some of our friends reject the open adoption concept. They're irretrievably invested in the theory of turning your back on the life event and never returning. Not so strangely, one of them is an adoptive mother herself. The other is a cousin whose undergraduate years included an unwanted pregnancy. They can't seem to recognize the wonderfulness of what we have. Maybe they just don't want to deal with the conflicts in their own hearts.

## June 2005

Emma is nine. We just spent a lovely visit with her and Dale. Jim couldn't come because of a work crisis. They came to Southern California, where we now live in Orange County. Holly moved to San Diego last year. Since we moved, the family get-togethers have been limited, but these ten days were great. Emma spent two nights on a sleepover at Holly's apartment. Dano was there for only three days and had to go back to work in Tempe, but those three days found Emma glued to his hip. They share a love for a Talking Heads music video, "Stop Making Sense," among other things.

Dale and Jim continue to show unbelievable generosity and comfort in sharing their daughter with what has become a very close, extended family. When we were living in Holliston, we got together six to eight times a year, plus a few stop-ins. Now we can't, but the feelings are as strong as ever.

Our open adoption is clearly a success. Our unique situation was created by Jim and Dale, who welcomed us into their lives. That's not at all a requirement of the process, but a choice they made that we embraced with respect. Open adoption is an opportunity. Like all opportunities, you make of them what you will. We've all spoken at workshops and been volunteers, trying to mentor others through the process. The more we see, the more we realize how special family building can really be.

## October 2013

Daniel is married and lives in Sydney, Australia making a living as a musician. Holly moved to San Diego and runs a thriving daycare business from her home. She started her own family and just celebrated her beautiful son's seventh birthday. Emma was a semi-finalist for the Robert Creeley Student Poetry Prize in her junior year of high school where she met her personal writing idol Naomi Shihab Nye. In Emma's sixteenth year Jim and Dale divorced. Dale lives in a three-bedroom condo nearby their old house that Jim now occupies.

Despite her exceptional writing skills, Emma told me she was having trouble putting her feelings at her 17th birthday into words.

Open Adoption means no secrets. There is no secret to the reality that all we can do is try. Then try again. So we do.

# Love is the real currency of our lives

We received our seed money to begin our journey from our parents. Then we married and shared what little we had with each other.

We invested our wealth in our children, where we see interest compounded daily.

The dividends are plentiful.

In guiding our day-to-day decisions, we check the ledger and hope for the best. It usually happens.

When we considered our most unusual investment eleven years ago, whose smile we thought we'd never see, there was a kind of alien warmth that tickled our souls.

Offering a grandchild who would illuminate the empty rooms of an unknown lovely young couple's life must be a gesture of ultimate philanthropy. If the gift were ours alone to give, it would not have happened.

Our seventeen-year-old son took the reins that were

*rightfully his to share. He and his sixteen-year-old lovemate made the choice, and we lived with that action and the expected parabola of emptiness and fullness it was to create in two disparate families.*

*My son Daniel and Holly forced open the doors of selfless love and sharing allowing the light of a higher awareness to shine through and brighten our spirit. It was a level of love that was new to us;*

*We thought it to be a love with no reward to see or feel, ever.*

*We learned to understand what giving really means.*

*We wanted so much to embrace it: the idea of giving away your grandchild?*

*We never would have approached that higher level of wealth without the chance to share giving so selflessly.*

*Love is a reverse kind of currency. The more we gave away, the richer we became.*

*At first it was an odd and awkward gesture. It took practice to create comfort. Lots of practice. Actually, more like on-the-job training.*

*At first there are expectations.*

*After the first few offerings, the expectations are diminished, then disappear.*

*It became cleaner and easier without these tails of anxiety.*

*The freedom of giving love with no consequence expected makes for the larger return.*

*The less you expect, the more you get. It seems to be a growing contradiction.*

## ... marbles ...

The more you give, the more you get. The less of an expectation of return, the greater that return. It's an Alice in Wonderland kind of logic. But it works, and we've learned it from our children, our greatest investments.

Over eleven years, the metaphor of our lives has grown in complexity as our children grow beside us and reflect ourselves back at ourselves.

Like a fun house hall of mirrors.

An oblique angle here, a subtle nuance uncovered there. A backward glance reveals the future just as peering ahead illuminates the past.

There is much to learn and discover through our son, new daughter, and grandchild. They teach us the lessons most valuable in our search for happiness and fulfillment.

They are the real gifts we have received ... from whom? We don't know.

So it seemed appropriate that the soul of that gift be offered as another gift to people we never expected to know.

Could the great contradiction continue?

Could this be the greatest gift possible?

Could there be a greater return?

No. No, that is not to be expected.

We must remember our lessons and give freely. Just as freely as our tears that flow at 4 AM.

# Cancerous truck driver

*Dear Jerry*

*Last Friday, a sixty-six-year-old French Canadian long-haul trucker fell asleep at the wheel with his young grandson next to him and drove over a van parked in the breakdown lane, killing three children and two grandparents. The thirty-year-old mother and father are in critical condition. Neither the truck driver nor his grandson was hurt. The initial headlines generated the usual outrage. The follow-up story told of the facts that the truck driver's thirty-five-year-old son, also a truck driver, had been killed in January when his truck was struck by a train. The guy's wife was institutionalized with Alzheimer's, and he was scheduled for surgery for prostate cancer on Wednesday.*

*The outrage has turned to pathos. I wouldn't guess that the thirty-year-old husband and wife would share in the pathos if and when they awake. It occurred to me that if the truck driver had run over the van first and then incurred all the ensuing* personal misery, there would be an attitude of "he got what he deserved." But when the sequence is reversed, it's confusing.

It seems that what's going on today has a greater degree of impact than what happened yesterday.

For the past year, I have been stopped in the halls of the nursing home on at least a weekly basis by people telling me how wonderful and devoted our father was. I heard it from the fellow visitors as well as the nurses. I didn't tell them that he spent 1945–1964 brutalizing his children. I wanted to.

I didn't tell them that any female that ever went to the bathroom in our house or took a shower could count on a visit from him. I didn't tell them that he once fucked my older brother's girlfriend for the price of a $500 used car. I thought all those things.

I didn't point out to them that, although he visited every single day, his motivation had as much to do with getting a free lunch meal as it involved visiting my mother. I didn't point out that when he fed her he was so insensitive as to stuff her mouth to the gagging point every time. I didn't point out that when he brushed her hair he would start brushing with steel-stiff bristles at about the middle of her forehead, raising a trail of little skinny red welts. I didn't point out how he'd pull back her covers and nightgown to expose the rash she had on her groin for anyone to examine. I neglected to tell them that when he brushed her teeth he just about choked her by jamming the toothbrush down her throat.

They didn't want to hear any of that. They wanted to admire a

devoted old man and believe that in the final years of a woman's
life her husband of fifty-six years came to visit her every single
day and fed her and brushed her hair and took care of her
in every way he could think of. They wanted to believe in a
hero figure. And they did. If you were to go into Avery Manor
tomorrow and mention his name on any floor, you would hear
the most extravagant tales of praise. They are all true. He did
all the things they say. No one else saw the detail, except me.
What is the reality?

He may have had mixed motivation in his constant
attendance. But there was definitely a mixture there. There
was some goodness in the motivation. To me, he was clearly
trying to atone. He was also bored and hungry. I saw that. No
one else did.

At this point in time, you and I are the only ones in the whole
world who really know of the monster. My wife, Carol, has
heard his history and seen his current actions. She knows
what a pig he is. She can only take our word for the horror. My
kids are in a similar situation. You and I are the only ones who
can know what happened forty years ago. To the rest of the
world, he is a slightly obnoxious old man. If they spend one
meal with him, they will probably not spend another. But that is
the extent of it. What is the reality?

Despite your extremely painful remarks to me in regard to
the motivation for my own feelings and despite your claim that
I don't know who you are and your clear warnings to keep quiet,
I go forward with the above narration. I believe you are making

a terrible mistake. I believe that my pain at not having you at mother's funeral is matched by yours at not being there. If that's not true, then I truly don't know who you are, and you can just disregard all of this as useless typing from a delusional fool. Mother was the only person in this world who loved you unconditionally, and though she clearly caused you and me harm, it was not intentional. No more than that the Canadian truck driver killed that family on purpose. They're still dead.

What happens today is important. I was surprised at your query in regard to how dad was doing. You asked twice. If you decided to come back for a visit I'm quite sure he would pay for your airfare with little hesitation. He has said several times that although your absence hurt, he could not muster up the hatred he had years ago. He seemed to almost want to, but couldn't.

He is not 'a new man'. He is significantly less dangerous. He still says the hurtful things. He really doesn't know any better. You should have seen him with Uncle Irving. I heard Irving moaning, "Harry, you're pulling off old scabs." He then went into the den looking for a drink and only found some ancient crème de menthe. But he laughed it off, in part because he also has some fond memories of Dad that counterbalance the ugliness.

Dad clearly knows how to attack. I believe he often attacks without even knowing it. I've repeatedly warned Carol and the kids to be on guard, and I haven't been wrong. If you should choose to encounter him, he will unquestionably say hurtful things. That is what he does. How hurtful he is depends in large

*part on your own attitude. I hope you will consider returning
for a visit.*

*I sat with Mother as she died. I sat with her the last eight
hours, holding her hand, kissing her forehead, and whispering
in her ear. Five minutes before she stopped breathing, I saw a
vapor-like substance escape from her mouth over a period of
about three seconds. It did not fill the room, though it seemed it
could have. It disappeared from sight. I believe it was her spirit.
I was about eighteen to twenty-four inches from her face and
saw it clearly. I won't try and relate to you the visitor Lisa had in
her bedroom that night. I'll let her tell you if you choose to hear.*

*I feel even more strongly than I did a year ago that it is well
worth your while to discover some level of peace. Despite
having been clearly warned by you twice to mind my own
business, I choose not to obey. I choose to tell you to come
home and find some way to overcome all of that hurt and
anger. You've got to try. If you feel as you did a year ago, you can
Xerox that same letter and send it again. It certainly made your
feelings quite clear. You couldn't do a better job.*

*But I believe what I am telling you as much as I have ever
believed anything in the last forty-nine years. He is who he is.
But you must become who you will be. It's just never too late.*

*Love,*
*Bobby*

# Father

## Orphans have no baggage

ORPHANS HAVE NO BAGGAGE. No expectations to live up to, no reputations to live down, and no parents to bury, literally or emotionally, despite a kind of holographic heritage.

The emptiness is like the ache lurking in an abscessed wisdom tooth. That emptiness causes unique pain artificially calmed by an amalgam filling or the tooth is likely just extracted. Extraction is not an option outside the dental metaphor. Or is it?

At 4 AM, on January 15, 2000, the phone rang three times before I awoke, picked it up to hear my wife 2700 miles away telling me that my father had died.

It was just one day *after* my fifty-third birthday. My mother had died just one day *prior* to my brother's fifty-third birthday. But he was in Japan, and with the time difference it could have actually been on his birthday. I could never figure that one out, but it was my first thought when my wife hung up. Second was the uncooked chicken breast in the fridge at my rented condo.

I'd cook it up with some Dijon honey mustard and bring it on the plane back to Boston. I'd need to pack a bit.

Flying on frequent-flyer miles made it easy to reschedule. That was when the frequent-flyer program was truly a benefit and flexible enough to accommodate their Gold Card customers with a sense of value. It's just a memory now, with change fees and limited seats; Gold Card privileges have evaporated and gone forever. I could get a nice fresh French bread roll at the Ralphs on the corner of Grand Avenue to make a sandwich. I decided at the last minute to include a crisp kosher gherkin and freshly sliced tomato in an efficient, sealable baggie.

Burying him seemed a bit anticlimactic. There was a short graveside ceremony in the frigid New England winter with a rabbi who mispronounced his name and didn't know he had three brothers. The only entertainment factor was a drop of clear mucous that hung from the tip of his nose throughout the four-minute eulogy. I'm sure every one of the twelve people gathered was more focused on that than anything he said. Other than the blushing bride, nobody there had ever met him. I guess the rabbi got his info from her, his second wife of only thirteen months – just long enough for the Massachusetts marital inheritance laws to kick in.

She had transported him by VanCar from the psychiatric ward of the Newton-Wellesley hospital to Newton City Hall where a justice of the peace qualified her for the $2.5 million estate he had inherited from my mother just four years previous.

The new Mrs. had pretty well sealed off all communication

between him and me for the past year. She didn't have to work at it. I wasn't calling much. The $2.5 million didn't bother me much, but the fact that they had pillaged all the funds from a trust account my mother had set up for my two children really pissed me off. I spent a year and $20,000 in legal fees fighting to get that back for them. The rabbi at the graveside was apparently instructed not to speak with me. Not a problem.

Father had always played the Dominant in life.

# 50 Shades of Grey, condos, and the Arab spring
## The morality of relationships

MORE THAN TEN MILLION READERS have set publishing sales records for *50 Shades of Grey*, creating a whole new genre dubbed "mommy porn." The book is simply more than a style of pornography for middle-aged women. The overriding theme is about Dominants and Submissives. This is what sets it apart from *Deep Throat*, the Kama Sutra, *Peyton Place*, and the like. The dominant-submissive theme differentiated it and propelled it to instant fame in numbers impossible to ignore.

The theme is well articulated in the first pages and oft repeated. To be clear, there is an extraordinarily large population of human beings who find the submissive role attractive, even essential. Without plagiarizing, it needs to be explained that the attractiveness of being a submissive is not the pain, but the emotional security. The essence of it is that trading a little bit of physical pain or discomfort is well worth the comfort of knowing the dominant is making you safe by controlling you and your environment. There are at least ten million readers out there who like the idea of somebody else taking responsibility for their comfort and their every decision. The submissive doesn't think or decide. The submissive is safe and secure.

While it's tempting to share a bit of the detail the author provides regarding how minimal amounts of pain or discomfort can be sexually stimulating, that's just not the point. The driving theme is that there are millions of people who don't want control over their lives. Let somebody else handle it. A little discomfort is well worth the price. Just look at the way condominiums are run! No joke.

Condominium and homeowner association dwellers give up almost total control of their homes and lifestyles to a board of dominants who make all the decisions. The HOA homeowner has no practical control. It is nothing like a democracy. In case you hadn't noticed, the HOA industry is alive and well in this country.

Much of the rest of the world has been ruled by monarchs, oligarchs, dictators, or any other label you choose to describe an authoritarian society where "the people" do what they are told. They have a measure of security and give up "freedoms" that US citizens believe they enjoy. Yes, there are some of us who truly want freedom to choose and are willing to take responsibility for our choices. But we are a minority.

A similar dynamic occurs in the workplace where there are *owners* and *employees*. The housing industry has the *landlord* and *tenant*. One group makes the rules and takes responsibility for the outcome. The other group does what they're told in a controlled environment

In North Africa, there appears to be an uprising against the authoritarian rule in place for millennia. A few young folks, informed by Facebook, Twitter, and all the iterations of the cyber age, want to make their own decisions about their own lives. They have that right, I guess. But they simply don't know how.

Representative democracy may appear to work in the United States, albeit with great difficulty and questionable results, but it is not so easy to create or transplant. Iraq was certainly a productive example of just how bloody the failed effort can be. Our august and revered Forefathers called it "The Great Experiment." It's still a work in progress within our borders.

To clarify this position, it's essential that we separate our government, a democratic republic, from our economic system, free-market capitalism. They are two different facets of our lifestyle that are conflated 100 percent of the time. That is a separate and worthwhile discussion. The point of *50 Shades* is that being a submissive is a free choice made by millions, maybe billions. China and the societies of the Far East have operated that way for almost all of recorded history. Ummmm, does the structure of the Catholic Church resonate here at all?

Dominant or submissive is a lifestyle choice made by most humans. Quite a small minority elect to take individual responsibility. They ought to be allowed that choice, but it just can't be forced upon the world as our government believes is our manifest destiny. Spreading democracy across the planet is and will continue to be about as effective as the War on Drugs, the War on Poverty, and all the friendly phrases that ill-informed dominants call up to justify their dominance.

There should be a middle ground. There doesn't seem to be. When submissives are forced to take responsibility for themselves, they often fail, and the society suffers and fails as well. Can you feel that "clench" way down deep?

# How Harold Brown survived a $635 million Chapter 11 bankruptcy

How did he turn a $635 million bankruptcy in 1990 into a $1.4 billion company in 2013? Read between the lines.

"WHEN THEY EXAMINED OUR RECORD of cash management and our policies on maintaining the properties, the banks found that in the past several years we had pumped $75 million back into our buildings. We don't have luxury offices. I don't have villas in Spain or fancy cars. They saw that we were doing business the right way, and that gave them confidence to continue dealing with us," said Harold Brown in a conversation about his historic emergence from a Chapter 11 bankruptcy that rocked the financial and real estate communities in New England. Thirty-three banks had entered into the Chapter 11 negotiations with Harold Brown, and after nearly three years, just three emerged, along with Harold.

## ... marbles ...

The Tax Reform Act of 1986 is often credited with creating the initial economic downward spiral that resulted in the tornado of economic chaos that characterized the early 1990s as it spread from New England across the country and from the real estate industry to the banks and the business communities that relied on those banks. Because tax advantages were removed, investors backed off from the booming New England real estate market, leaving hundreds of defaulted mortgages that had been created with 5 percent down payments or, for some creative investors, no cash at all. The famous 3-2-1 mortgage buydowns that were prevalent in the late 1980s created a vacuum of equity on the buyer side. Deregulated banks had become accustomed to giving brief scrutiny to real estate loans and generating huge profits. They fell victim to borrowers who abandoned their overpriced properties when they realized they had no equity left. The market had ceased its 25–35 percent annual appreciation. The banks were left with huge losses, and those losses impacted their good loans as FDIC personnel invaded New England and began running the banks out of business.

The biggest question asked by most observers was "Why?"

Why did Brown go into a $635 million Chapter 11 that cost over $10 million in legal fees for his side alone?

Why would he allow his properties to fall into the hands of a bankruptcy trustee?

Why would he give up the most important ingredient in business – control?

First you have to understand the mind of Harold Brown.

I grew to know him well over 20 years of writing about real estate. Harold has unshakable confidence and always maintains control to insure that confidence is rewarded. At no time did he or his associates ever consider this anything other than a *reorganization*. The word 'bankruptcy' and all its conotations was just never a part of this process. Other than its legal ramifications and new rules. Harold was dealing with a business situation with the driving force being to maximize profits within the legal guidelines presented. If you're thinking *bankruptcy*, then your mind isn't right. Harold's mind is always right. That might be why 20 years later the Boston Globe did an updated profile on him in 2013. At age 88 they had his holdings "pegged at $1.4 billion" combining 5500 residential units with two and a half million square feet of commercial space.

## Back to the *restructuring* story in Harold's words

"We had begun a consensual restructuring. We had to. With the way the real estate industry and the entire business community was going in '90 and '91 we had to do something unusual to continue. We wanted very much to avoid Chapter 11 because of the expense and the loss of control. We negotiated with all of the banks we did business with. None of them were very happy, but they responded as business people should in difficult times."

What were some of the things Brown looked for in renegotiating with nearly fifty banks and financial institutions?

"We were hoping for forgiveness on certain amounts that

were just untenable. We offered them a percent ownership in the properties in return so that they could potentially benefit in the long term. These 'hope certificates,' as they are often called, can turn out to be valueless if the reorganization fails or if the property never recovers. In our situation, the banks had every reason to believe that we could pull out of it. Certain portions of the loans were deferred. There's a French term called 'tranche' that describes a process where a given nonperforming loan is split into two loans. Part is restructured to allow payments to be made and a return to the performing category. The other part is considered nonperforming and written off or written down. This allows the lender to salvage some value out of what would otherwise be a total loss."

Some industry experts say that Brown strong-armed the banks into giving him deals that others could never have gotten.

"We made deals that made sense for everybody. If there was any arm-twisting going on, it was the economy that put pressure on us all. Real estate was in a tailspin, and it was carrying the rest of the economy with it. Federal regulators invaded New England and imposed unreasonable and often foolish rules that forced many good solvent companies out of business. We tried to be creative and survive. We had done business with most of these banks for decades and paid them millions of dollars in interest and fees over that period. We weren't first-time home buyers looking for a deal. Business can be a place where hard decisions have to be made. The proof is that most every bank agreed to some kind of restructuring. All except the Bank of New England."

The pivotal reason given for filing the Chapter 11 was the intransigence of the Bank of New England. According to Brown, they stonewalled the negotiations and put liens on all the properties they were involved with. After a ninety-day period, the liens became "priority liens" and fouled the entire process. There was no other choice for Brown and his partners but to file for protection for their sake and for the sake of the other creditors. At that time, there could be no way of knowing that the process would drag on for so many years and cost $10 million in legal fees.

Why would Bank of New England be so intransigent? Why would all the other banks cooperate? It is rumored that the Bank of New England was already in trouble with the FDIC and the government regulators would not allow them to negotiate at all. They insisted that no assets could be written down because that would put the critical asset-to-loan ratios out of proper proportion and result in the bank's closing. The bank was caught between Harold Brown and the FDIC.

"We put about 10 percent of our properties into Chapter 11. We selected those properties that the Bank of New England was involved with and worked out other arrangements on 90 percent of our holdings," explained Brown.

Didn't the idea of $10 million in legal fees unsettle Brown?

"You have to understand that the $10 million cost is ultimately borne by the banks. That's $10 million that would have been available to use in the settlement and restructuring. The lawyers didn't take it from me. They took it from the banks.

And that doesn't count all the legal expenses the banks incurred. It must have equaled or exceeded our own expenses."

Harold Brown is best known as Boston's largest real estate owner and manager of residential and commercial property. He also was a partner in Northeastern Mortgage and University Bank. Over the decades he's had extensive involvement with city, state, and federal government agencies. None of that experience prepared him for dealing with the bankruptcy proceedings.

"At the beginning of the process, I found myself sitting in a crowded room with a hundred attorneys and had no idea what was going on. I relied heavily on our own attorney, Bob Somma, from Goldstein & Manello. He has a good business sense and was cost-conscious. Ross Honig was involved as well. The endless discussions could have put you to sleep. In one instance, they did. I was on a three-way conference call with my attorney and one of the many bank attorneys late one night and I actually dozed off. At times, this seemed like a process of attrition. Who could last the longest? Thirty out of thirty-three banks didn't make it."

What were some of the machinations and maneuverings that went on?

"I couldn't begin to summarize all the offers and counteroffers that took place over the five years. There were hundreds. Some that come to mind were the simplest. The initial offer from Bank of New England that persuaded us to file for Chapter 11 sticks out. They offered us six months forbearance on the loans, and then if everything wasn't up-to-date, they would take over all the properties. This was in 1991. We knew things were just starting to get bad and that offer was without any merit. We did what we had to in order to protect ourselves and the other creditors. We've been doing business in this community for many years and were very sensitive to the needs of our smaller suppliers. We didn't want to see them become victims of the filing. Prior to the bankruptcy, we were able to make sure that all of those small creditors, those under $2000, were paid in full.

"Another interesting segment of the proceedings focused on a package of properties all covered by one blanket mortgage of $120 million. We were forced to give it back to the bank. The bank wrote it down to $40 million and took an $80 million loss. They then turned around and sold the package for $80 million to show a $40 million profit. We were the buyers. In essence we were able to trade in a group of properties that were over mortgaged and get them back on very favorable terms. It was a high point in the proceedings.

"Looking at the whole process, we were able to get rid of a lot of nonperforming properties with poor cash flow and restructure the good ones for a profitable future. We were able to get out from under about $250 million in debt. We are operating on a stronger basis now than we were before. That's the purpose of reorganization. Our only lingering problem was that we had more accountants in our offices than property managers. We had eighty people in our offices before the Chapter 11, and we had eighty people after, except afterward we had twenty more accounting people. The reporting requirements of a Chapter 11 are very burdensome."

One of the traits Harold Brown is best known for is his ability to focus on a specific topic or goal without being encumbered by fuzzy nonessential issues. In asking him to describe the bankruptcy process, he responded in characteristic style.

"There are eleven building blocks that are essential to the understanding of the process.

"The first is *open disclosure*. You must be forthcoming with the banks, creditors, and bankruptcy trustee on exactly what your assets really are. If they find out later on in the process that you are trying to hide something, you lose your credibility." What kind of credibility can you have once you've filed for bankruptcy? "That's all you have left," offered Brown. "If you expect to get through the process successfully, you have to think that way. If you think that all is lost and you try to hide assets and be less than forthright, you'll probably lose. We chose to fully disclose and play for the win. We maintained our credibility with the trustee in charge and survived the process. I'd recommend that others do the same."

The second building block that Brown identified was a *level playing field*. "All the banks and creditors must have the same opportunity to recover their funds. You can't favor one over the other, even if one is being more cooperative. It was frustrating to us because many of the bankers were more than willing to work with us while others were just contrary and obstinate. They all got the same opportunity to get their share of the assets."

The third item on the list is *cross-collateralization*. "While this is common practice in real estate financing, it's not allowed in the bankruptcy proceedings. Previous loan structures that are set up in this fashion are acceptable, but no new deals can be structured this way in the bankruptcy proceedings. Every property has to stand on its own."

The *restructuring loan* is an important ingredient. "At the beginning of the process, we tried to estimate the legal and collateral costs of going through the bankruptcy. We estimated the costs would be $20 million. The creditors figured it would be $2 million. The trustee decided on $10 million, which turned out to be quite accurate.

"Stan Miller had been named trustee at the outset. The banks submitted three names. We submitted three names, and Stan was chosen. He was one of the names offered by the banks, and he turned out to be an excellent choice.

"All the banks had to make an additional loan totaling $10 million to cover the legal costs. They each contributed based on their share of the claim. This is a good example of how the creditors can end up losing even more than they might have to. We worked part of our troubles out in a consensual restructuring that had little legal cost and provided more assets for our creditors. If it weren't for the Bank of New England personnel, we could have saved close to $10 million in expense they wouldn't have had to deal with."

The *forbearance period* is the fifth building block of the process. Brown asked for eight years. The banks wanted it to be one. The compromise was four years with the banks having the option of extending it for another four years if they felt it was to their benefit. "As I sensed the market was turning, it was strongly requested that an additional four years or even two years be extended as it would increase the value of their 25 percent contingency fee. The banks refused, perhaps due to regulatory pressure. This request was denied, and the forbearance period terminated. It was my estimate that the banks gave up some $150 million in value. This part of the negotiations required long, involved, and expensive forecasting of what the economy might do. It was a tedious and confusing period with everyone trying to predict the future. While it was a necessary step, I feel it could have been done in a more effective manner that took less time and money," suggested Harold.

*Pay rate per property* is the next part of the process. "There was a schedule of debt payoffs for each of the properties that had to be maintained. If the schedule was missed, there was what's called a *default rate*. What the premise focused on was that we had to make regular predictable payments on each of the buildings to satisfy the creditors that we were doing as promised. If we missed a single payment, they would demand the whole amount to be repaid. There was absolutely no comingling allowed. Each property had to stand on its own, so there was really nowhere to go if the payment couldn't be made. The foolish part was that if we could have repaid the loan, we would have. If we were late on a payment, it meant there was no money. If there was no money, then the bank would want all the money? It made no sense. It was like the eighteenth-century physicians who practiced 'bleeding' as a cure. If the patient didn't recover after they had a pint of blood extracted, then they'd extract another and then another until the patient was dead. This was what the default rate was all about. We ended up losing about 20 percent of the properties this way.

"There was another interesting feature of the pay rate. By putting money back into the properties in the form of capital improvements, we could earn a *pay rate credit*. This means that by improving the property, the mortgage got reduced. It was like getting double-duty out of the cash flow. It was a strong incentive to maintain and improve the properties and a disincentive to let them fall into disrepair. This helped us and gave the banks confidence that their assets were being well maintained. "

Associated with this concept is the seventh building block called *reserves for tenant improvements and capital improvements*. "We were allowed to maintain reserves for improvements out of the positive cash flow of each property.

The *excess cash flow* beyond what was put aside for reserves was to be used to pay down the loans on each specific property. These funds were strictly property specific, and there was no comingling allowed."

The next ingredient in the process is the *default note*, which would come into effect if everything was not resolved in the four-year forbearance period.

A major and important part of the process was the part that allowed for *selective retained assets*. "This was my incentive for good behavior. I was allowed to select certain properties that I could keep for my own and continue to survive. I was allowed to draw $1 million a year from these properties. I used this revenue to buy back many of the properties that were going through the bankruptcy. In effect, they allowed me to continue to earn a living, and the result was that what I was able to earn actually found its way back to the bankruptcy creditors in a roundabout way. It was a facet of the procedure that benefited everybody. I was allowed this opportunity based on my continued cooperation with the process."

This seemed to be a key component in Harold's ability to come out of the bankruptcy in a viable condition. He naturally selected the best properties as retained assets and then bought back the best of what was left with his earnings. He likened it to General MacArthur's Pacific strategy in World War II. After Pearl Harbor, he didn't start on our side of the Pacific and work his way west. He went all the way across the ocean to hit the main Japanese bases and knock out some of their supply lines and then came back to mop up what was left.

After the four-year period of reorganization, all the good properties had been retained, and the bad ones were eliminated. The final batch of properties were packaged and bought by Brown for $3 million. During the process, he had bought up some of the default notes so that he actually owned about one-third of the notes himself. This resulted in $1 million of the final $3 million going back to him. He bought up part of the *deficiency loans* for two reasons. First, he didn't want some of the more antagonistic and mean-spirited creditors involved in the process, so he bought their shares. Second, he was in a better position to make that final offer.

The final piece of the puzzle is the *contingency fee*, which turned out to be 25 percent of the net capital gain that might be made on the property for the next thirty years. This was projected at approaching $5 million. Harold bought it up for $1.2 million to help the cash going to the creditors and to cut any strings to his future opportunities.

As noted, those *future opportunities* grew to $1.4 billion, and counting. Survival in any arena is about getting your mind right. Mortality? Immortality? It's all about what's going on right now and what you can do to control your future. Leave the rest to the historians to judge.

# Heaven; hope

## January 15, 1997

Dear Dano,

*I was sitting with Joe, our new Florida Associate Publisher, in a car outside a client's office in Boca Raton, waiting for one of our new salespeople to emerge. Joe's a real nice, levelheaded guy from Brooklyn whose father was a successful butcher. His older brother is a Chassidic rabbi, and his younger brother is a race car fanatic. Joe seems to be the reasonable one in the middle. I like him a lot.*

*We sat patiently waiting, chatting about business in general, when he paused and said, "I want to ask you something you really don't have to answer if you don't want to. You made a comment earlier about 'praying to God' for something. Do you believe in God? I mean, do you believe in the next life and heaven and hell?"*

*I smiled and responded quickly, "I absolutely do. It may not be the God with the big white beard or the heaven with the* angels flying around in pillowcases, but I absolutely believe that there is a superior being and that there is a heaven. In fact, I'm sure of it."

Joe smiled warmly and said, "You're sure of it?" He chuckled. "You must have had something happen to you or seen something to be so sure."

"I've had several things happen to me over the past few years, and, yes, I'm certain that there is more to our existence than what we wake up to each day. I won't bother going through the details of my own personal experiences. It's not like the X-Files or anything, but it's a very comfortable, secure feeling that there's more to life than selling ads. There's more reason to try and do the right thing than the immediate reward or punishment you get from your actions. I believe in the soul. I believe in the evolution of the soul. I believe that there is God inside all of us."

"And what about heaven and hell? Do you believe in that?"

"I certainly believe in heaven. In fact, I'm certain that this is heaven, where we are right now."

He laughed again and said, "Tell that to my wife. She's waiting to win the lottery. How can you say that this is heaven? Look at all the misery. Look at the wars and the disasters. Look at AIDS. How can this be heaven? If this is heaven, I'd hate to see what hell might be like."

"It's both," I said. "Heaven is the chance to be happy. It's not a place where you have all the wealth in the world and all the food and women and creature comforts right at hand.

*That's not heaven. That's not even good here on earth. Joy and happiness don't come from having all those things. It comes from having the opportunity to obtain them through our own efforts and the satisfaction that goes along with knowing you achieved them. That's true heaven, the sense of achievement, self-worth, and self-respect that comes from struggling and succeeding."*

*"What about that guy sitting on the corner panhandling for quarters? Is it heaven for him too?" Joe asked.*

*"Of course it is. He has the same opportunity we all have. He's just not taking advantage of it. Maybe he has a little piece of hell right now: hopelessness.*

*"But it can change. And that's what makes heaven. The chance for failure and misery is right there alongside the chance for success and happiness. If it weren't, the success and happiness wouldn't be worth anything. If everybody had everything they wanted, it would all be taken for granted, unappreciated, and therefore worth nothing and bring no satisfaction. The fact that you have to struggle to be happy is what makes happiness exist. What good is having a million dollars if everybody else has it too?"*

*"I don't agree. I would definitely like to win the Lotto. I'm sure that I will be much happier and lead a much finer life if my wife and my two daughters could all share in about $15 million. You're crazy if you think different. You're just not being realistic. The theory sounds nice and intellectual, but I'd like to see what you'd do if somebody handed you $10 million. I doubt you'd*

refuse."

"No, I wouldn't refuse, but I wouldn't expect my life to be any happier than it is now. In fact, I'm sure it would be less happy. With any windfall like that, there are expectations. They would come from within me, from my wife, my kids, and my friends. Everybody would be expecting something. It's not just that I might share it with them, but I would have expectations of myself.

"With all that money, shouldn't I go out and do something productive? Look what Pulitzer did. Look at Carnegie, Mellon, Nobel. They all went out and formed institutions with their wealth that live on and make the world better. Shouldn't I do that too? Then I would have to go out and use that money wisely to accomplish those goals. And to tell you the truth, I'm not such a great businessman or financial sharpie. I'd probably end up blowing most of it and getting taken in by some really clever con men, and then how would I feel?

"I'd be a failure. My wife and kids would look and see how I had failed. They'd be ashamed and disappointed. Maybe I wouldn't give them as much as they wanted. Maybe they'd think they should have a chance to spend a few million. Maybe they'd be angry and resentful that I didn't give them a chance to try. Maybe some of the people I shared the money with would feel that I was not gracious in the way I gave them money. Maybe they thought I was being condescending. Maybe those who I considered friends are no longer my friends because of jealousy. I'm not the most diplomatic or tactful guy. People have *their own sensitivities. I'm sure I'd offend somebody.*

*"And what would I do with all that money that would make me happier? I wouldn't buy a bigger house. It would just mean more to clean and furnish and worry about. I wouldn't buy a bigger car. I don't even like cars. I'd probably go out and spend it on great rich food and die of a cholesterol attack in about three weeks. I'm sure my wife would go out and buy a ton of clothes, and then what? Buy more clothes? I could pay for my daughter's grad school tuition. That would be nice. But you know when she went through undergrad and paid for half herself and we paid for half, there was a great feeling of teamwork and accomplishment. That wouldn't be there. Then when she graduated and we had about $20K in loans to pay off, her grandfather made a gift to her of the money to pay off those loans. It was the most generous thing he'd ever done. For him it was a mitzvah. For us it was a great event.*

*"If we had all that money, none of that happiness would have happened. I am absolutely convinced that $15 million would be far more harmful than good. No, I wouldn't refuse it, but I'd sure be real quiet about it and probably never spend it. Money is not happiness. Having everything you need is not heaven. Earning what you need is heaven. Struggling and failing and struggling some more gives us the sense of self-worth that is so much more important than anything else in this world. Struggling with temptation strengthens us. Without temptation, we'd have no moral fiber. That relates to the evolution of the soul that I mentioned."*

**... marbles ...**

The salesperson we were waiting for came out of the office, and our conversation was over. Joe closed with, "I'm still buying my Lotto tickets tonight. I'd like just a small taste of some of those problems."

Love,
Daddo

# Simply the worst moment of my entire life

### Frontiers of marriage and family

## September, 1990

THEY SAY THAT WORLD'S FALL APART. So do marriages. Mine did in September of 1990. It didn't really fall apart. Dissolved is more accurate. We'd been together twenty seven years, since high school, and then we weren't. Not even close. We turned around and there was nothing there.

My wife told me that I would be the one to tell my seventeen year old daughter and my fourteen year old son that the world as they had known it thus far was now over. They sat at the kitchen table. My daughter ran screaming from the house into the gathering darkness of the early fall evening. My son decomposed where he sat in his chair where he used to munch giant bowls of Frosted Flakes.

Three hours later at 10 PM my wife deservedly threw my sorry ass out of the house with the back seat of my car piled with everything I owned. It was a small car. I still had room in the trunk.

It wasn't until December 28th of that same year that my house caught on fire in a New England snowstorm. I was in San Diego on a sales call and got the message from a secretary.

"Your house seems to be on fire." Is all she said, and handed me the phone. My daughter gave me the details calling from a neighbor's living room. Daniel had grabbed the hamster cage as they ran out. That was about all they had. My wife was rushing her way home from work driving through the blizzard.

I caught the next flight to Boston and met the family at the nearby Residence Inn. We decided it would be best for all concerned to try and examine the wreckage of our lives as well as the house. It took three months to get the house rebuilt. It took my wife and I almost two years of counseling to try and rebuild our family. Emotional damage is done to all and can't be repaired. You need to salvage what you can and rebuild. We're still working at it. Every day. That's really the only way.

None of us will ever forget. Emotional shrapnel remains embedded in each of us. In some small way that horrific series of events helped teach us the lessons we'd need when we discovered Emma. We had a different understanding of what 'family' meant, and what was at stake.

# Casey's Diner ain't what it used to be, or is it?

## Small town morality

*SOME QUESTIONS JUST DON'T seem to have answers. How come Ted Turner can give millions to prop up the United Nations and Bill Gates can give a billion to wipe out measles in Africa, yet the world still seems to be falling apart? There are more millionaires on this planet today than there were potato farmers in 19th-century Ireland. Why aren't things good and getting better? I need some answers here!*

Casey's Diner needs no introduction to those in the Greater Boston area. In the '60s and early '70s, an interesting group of old-timers spent their late afternoons at the far end of the counter. The oldest, a former plumber who was eighty-four at his death, spent a good hour nursing two "all-arounds," while the youngest, an active house painter in his late sixties, scarfed

115

down a fried egg sandwich on whole wheat in about the time
it took to serve the other three. Next to Joe & Nemos, Casey's
is the best-known name in New England for good hot dogs.
It's a third-generation place nestled on the outskirts of Natick
Square, home of Doug Flutie.

Casey's is the kind of place where celebrity does not bring a
bandwagon mentality. The folks at Casey's grew up with Dougie
and some with his father. They know him, his wife, and his
brother, Darren. They either liked him or didn't and haven't
changed their minds, regardless of any trophies, fame, or fortune.

The four late afternoon regulars didn't include names like
Getty or Rockefeller. All were either second-generation Irish or
Italian dressed in open collar white shirts. They chewed their
dogs, sipped their black coffee, and talked of what interested
them in low tones not overheard. Respect for privacy was a
basic value rarely breached back when Casey's was located on
Washington Street.

What was pretty commonly known, though not discussed,
was that this group of four, sometimes five, seniors cared about
their town and their people in a unique way. For the previous
twenty years, they had pooled what started to be a few dollars
each and bought some Christmas cheer for those locals less
fortunate. They would turn their backs on what today's media
has dubbed "the homeless" with all the cause célèbre that
accompanies popular fundraisers.

In the '60s, when the group first started helping out, the
targets of their generosity would have been called bums and

drunks. But they were *their* bums and drunks. The ones they went to grammar school with. The ones whose sister went out with Louie when Louie couldn't find a prom date to save his soul. There was no expectation that providing a hot meal, a few extra dollars, or an inexpensive gift was going to change the world. There was no goal to rehabilitate the homeless and create a better society. It was just a gesture at Christmastime to be a Christian and help out those that had less and would likely never have more.

The ambience at Casey's would never be called "ambience" by the counter trade. It's a place where the elderly ladies of the town are given a seat when they come in, and there's no blue language of any sort when a female is present. The hot dogs are automatically cut in half for the fairer sex in deference to dainty and to avoid the possible visual vulgarity of a lady biting on a whole hot dog.

There's a 1950's kind of morality at play inside the sliding front door of Casey's that is remarkably comfortable. The banter is light and open to all. Focus is mostly on the high school football or baseball teams, and more often than not comparing today's group with that of the great eleven in 1957 or the starting nine in 1962. State championships have far more panache than any Super Bowl or World Series. The seriousness of the discussion regarding the arm of this year's starting QB is of more import than whether Romney or Bulger will survive.

Over the years, the small group of Casey's deacons came to the point where the decades of hard work brought some of the men significant business success. They began distributing thousands of dollars, and not just at Christmas. It wasn't a fund drive kind of thinking. It was a few locals who understood that what goes around comes around. There was no publicity, nor would any be tolerated by the small group, now gone. They decided who got what and when. There's a small wing of the new library that bears no plaque, but it wouldn't exist without them. Widows found some additional financial support arriving in their mailbox long after the flowers from the wake had wilted. Some less fortunate local high school grads found their college textbooks paid for along with an activity fee or two. They weren't the athletes that you'd expect this group to support. No fancy clothes or cars. Nothing that the NCAA could consider an infraction. Just some commonsense help to the children of the community. No thanks asked for or expected. What goes around comes around.

There are many hot dog stands in Greater Boston. New England Speed sold a $4.50 kosher quarter pounder in the downtown meat district. There was Simcos on the Bridge in Mattapan, home of the famous foot-long dog, and there was the aforementioned Joe & Nemos, granddaddy of them all.

It's the hot dog that Casey's is famous for. Pat Casey will stand behind the counter by the copper steamer forking over your order with a genuine smile, but never say a word about the quiet old-timers. It was before his time. In a little yellow ten-seat diner outside Natick Square, there's more to chew on than Kayem franks in freshly steamed rolls.

See you there, but don't ask questions that have no answers.

# Graduation apology

## I'm sorry

GRADUATIONS ARE JUST a bore, one of life's chronic endurance tests. They are the hard-benched depots of our rites of passage through life's tacky journey. First, your own, then your kids', and then your grandkids'. Almost as torturous as dance recitals, I have never sat through a graduation that was anything but tedious.

My first experience was my own commencement from Hebrew School after six combative years. I can still remember the Talmudic phrase I had to learn to be a participant in that four-hour Saturday morning service back in May of 1960. From there, it was a junior high school ceremony, then a legitimate high school commencement on the football field of Newton North High, and then college commencement just about four years hence in the town of Amherst, Massachusetts.

It began again thirty years later with my two kids. My blessed daughter favored us with a master's degree that required both a graduation and convocation. My son, my only son, managed to graduate ASU after five and a half years of struggle that began at Framingham State, stopped at ASU, diverted to Mesa Community College, and then wound back to the grand campus of the Sun Devils for another double hit of graduation and commencement. After plodding through these 213 words, you know just how I felt sitting through that last two-hour commencement.

"Okay, already. I get it."

All 'valedictorian' means to me is one more stilted speech. I'm sorry. I really am. But I just have no patience for processions and Elgar's "Pomp and Circumstance." It makes me appreciate Iggy Pop.

Now it was 11 AM on Saturday morning and finally over. My twenty-two-year-old graduate was quite pleased as he litanized over each university building we passed by.

"I'll never have to sit in that damn lecture hall again.

"No more 8 AM classes in that building again.

"I'll never have to hunt for a parking spot in that lot ever again.

"That's the last time I'll drive by that bookstore in my whole life."

Yet he didn't take off his mortarboard with the left-hanging pink tassel until well after noon, and the maroon robe didn't come off until about 1:15. The four of us had a nice lunch at Ra, his favorite sushi bar, where his older sister reinforced her senior position by taking charge of the ordering just so the young graduate didn't get too carried away with all the attention.

## ... marbles ...

Younger brothers require constant reminders to preserve the peace and order of the clan.

Lunch was necessarily light in anticipation of the great graduation dinner planned for The Pointe, one of Phoenix's finer dining experiences, where we were sure to drop the equivalent of half a semester's tuition for wine, dinner, and Bananas Foster for four. There was a stop scheduled prior to dinner at a favorite professor's home for a quick drink and formal farewell. Once in a great while, you find a teacher in your path that leaves a mark on you forever. Dr. Madeline Williamson was that person in our son Daniel's life.

Dr. Williamson was the 'tough cop' on the beat who cared a great deal about the music she taught and even more about the students she taught it to. She brooked no excuses of "the dog ate my homework" variety and had little patience for those who had chosen music as their major but wouldn't put in the time to practice at the keyboard. Daniel had started off as one of those guys that had always gotten by on his smile, but he had met a stone wall with Dr. Williamson. She had read him the riot act early in their relationship two years ago and pointed out that she wouldn't hesitate to flunk his sorry, lazy ass if he didn't do his homework, and he damn well better show up for class on time with the lessons learned because she had better things to do than look at his straight-toothed, gleaming white smile.

Daniel used up his first two strikes with her within the first six days and was facing "the boot" if the third lesson wasn't satisfactory. He finally got the message, put in his time practicing, and hadn't missed a beat in the last two years. Dr. Williamson returned the favor with her own passionate instruction and encouragement that brought our Daniel to this day and this level of measurable talent in the performing arts. She wanted to wish Dano well before he fled the nest. Why not? We planned a forty-five minute, pre-dinner get-together at her home in Phoenix.

Daniel guided us through the lights of suburban Phoenix to her 1930's ranch-style home that overlooked a big public park. Now 1930's construction isn't such a big deal back in Boston where 18th & 19th-century architecture dominates with a flash of Graham Gund. But in Arizona, the land of Frank Lloyd Wright, 1930's is a vintage that is much appreciated. We were greeted by the loud barks of her three dogs considerately locked away for the moment and Dr. Madeline Williamson standing in the driveway with her fist filled with a glass of Wild Turkey on ice that needed a refill.

Dr. Williamson looked formidable with black horn-rimmed glasses in a de nouveau style I couldn't quite place. She had a smile to match Daniel's and an accent born in the farm country of Ohio, cultured on the campus of Ohio-Wesleyan, and generously seasoned with Chicago and New York "front of the mouth" fricatives. She gave Dano a big hug and shook all our hands with a warmth and sincerity that set the tone for our visit.

We filed into the living room of her ranch to view an extra-ordinarily decorated and cozy little room that bathed the visitor in subtle textures and bold primary colors against a background of earth tones. You had the sense that you had just entered "someplace." The art was a mixture of Erté, animated cartoon cels, and a few Old Masters. A background of classical piano on the CD player easily drowned out the fading yips of her canine housemates. She apologized that her partner, Brigitta, wasn't there to meet us, but she had to work at the bookstore that night.

Walking through the nickel tour, we stopped in the dining room where my daughter and I lightened the load with a well-chilled bottle of Bombay Sapphire. It had been in the freezer and reached that syrupy consistency most prized by the inveterate gin drinker. Madeline refilled her tumbler with a bit more Wild Turkey to be sociable. The kitchen retained the original '30's style cabinetry and even what looked like a vintage Formica and chrome kitchen table. We had salami roll-ups and a selection of olives to nibble on with what turned out to be "swimming pool style" baked Brie. It seems as though Madeline's glass of Wild Turkey might not have been her first as she nuked a small wheel of French brie for the second time and laughed along with the rest of us as she pulled it out in liquid form. This was actually a very special night for Dr. Williamson. Even more special than for Daniel.

We sat back down in the living room, and Madeline did a very articulate job of entertaining us with stories of her exploits in remodeling previous houses and her plans for this one. Her narrative had the precise speech and well-planned logic of a college professor who knew whereof she spoke and made it clear that regardless of whatever quantity of Wild Turkey may or may not have passed her lips, she was in full and competent control of the situation. We were having a great time. The CD changer switched to a softer etude.

She looked at my wife and I and said, "I want to tell you a small story about how your son affected my life and made an impression on me that I will never forget. He was there for me in my moment of need when all of my colleagues had left me alone."

"Oh?" we said as Madeline managed to hold eye contact with both of us simultaneously.

It seems that in this topsy-turvy world of the 21st century the students had gained ascendancy over the faculty insofar as if they didn't like their grade, they could complain to a "higher-up" and call into question the competency of the instructor, even if that instructor was a full professor with twenty-five years of academic experience and doctorate credentials. Dr. Williamson was well-known as an uncompromising bearer of the academic standards of her nationally respected music department. She was ready and willing to go the extra mile for her students, as she had done for our Dano, but the students had to show up, do their part, and learn their lessons. If not, there was really no alternative available.

It was during this most recent semester that, for the first time in twenty-five years, Madeline had been challenged by not one but two students who felt like flexing their political muscle in an environment that seemed to offer the nonperformer inordinate opportunity for redress. The strategy of each was not so much to question Dr. Williamson's judgment of their musical accomplishment, but to take the form of a personal attack on her character and veiled innuendo on her lifestyle. Her faculty colleagues quickly faded into the background when the challenge was brought to a jury of her peers. These same colleagues that had offered Cheshire cat grins of appreciation for the millions of dollars in grants she had won over her tenure of a quarter century chose meek silence in the face of the challenge of two nineteen-year-old underclasspersons.

Daniel was the only one to stand and be counted. It seems that he took the time to pen a letter to the head of the department, narrating his own personal experiences with Dr. Williamson and how her motivating style of instruction had enabled him to learn his lessons and earn the talent he now had. He supported her and disparaged the words of his lazy classmates for what they were. It seems that he was the only one to offer any kind of support.

The department head resolved the issue by supporting Dr. Williamson's grading decision, but gave the students a chance to retake the required class under the auspices of a less-challenging community college affiliate. It was not really much of a deal, except to Madeline. She had spent twenty-five years earning a reputation as an individualist who cared passionately about her music and her students. She understood the place of uncompromising standards in a world that had opted for the "go along to get along" mentality. She had found only one kindred spirit in her moment of trial, and it turned out to be our Daniel.

This was an episode in her life that she would remember. Daniel had made a difference.

She thanked him and handed him a hand-wrapped graduation gift of twelve classic jazz LPs from her own personal collection of favorites. Dan had tears in his eyes, not so much because of the shared love of jazz greats, but because he knew how precious the albums were to Madeline. There was nothing she could offer him of more personal value. Dr. Williamson remained dry-eyed in her professorial demeanor, but held onto that hug of gratitude for just an extra beat. I understood the need for the Wild Turkey. I remembered that three-line Talmudic verse from my own first graduation in May of 1960.

"If I am not for myself, who will be for me?
But if I am for myself alone, who am I?
And if not now, when?"

I guess Dano learned that lesson too. This seemed to be a graduation ceremony of a different texture.

# The Baja, the condo boardroom, and my '79 shovelhead

## Three days in the Baja on my old Hog

FIVE DIVERSE, INEXPERIENCED people surviving and succeeding on a condo association board is daunting. Having just spent three days on a motorcycle run through the Baja Desert peninsula with four new guy friends resonated with similarities. It truly takes all types, and the key is figuring out how to get along and use each other's assets while protecting the weak spots. Each condo board has individuals with a lot to offer. Too often their potential contribution gets left in the dust because of the inability of the group to function. Diversity is good. Being nonjudgmental and having a willingness to listen is vital.

I'm a born and bred Boston guy who got hooked up with a transplanted New Jersey guy, two native Southern Californians, and one guy who would never tell. Conflict? Maybe. The invitation to this jaunt came about a month ago from a fellow I had met through a friend of my wife. Bill Murphy was a long-time motorhead and always looking for somebody new to share an adventure.

"Hey, how about a guy's weekend in Mexico?" said Wild Bill.

"Why not?" said I.

Nothing to lose. Bill had three or four other guys who he thought would join us. Didn't matter much to me. I was just happy for an excuse to get in the saddle for three days in some strange new place. Bill was the big thinker – the idea man. He was a big old ex-marine, six foot three and three hundred pounds, with a short graying brush-cut, familiar with the Mexican jaunt who loved the outdoors.

Friday morning rolled around, and I rolled up to his house in Irvine to hear that two out of the original five had been replaced. The third, Jeff, Bill's pal of thirty years, was currently broken down on the way over to the jump-off point. Bill was heading out to rescue him and would be back in twenty minutes. The other two new guys should arrive soon. And off he went. Once Bill got a goal in mind, it didn't matter much what fell in his way. He was going for it. Single-minded focus and determination, with a license plate frame that said, "Danger builds character." You need guys like that.

Five minutes later, the two newbies pulled up, each riding late-model Harleys. One was that well-known "Full-Dresser" touring bike that weighs about eight hundred pounds soaking wet. It had just two hundred miles on it and was Dick's first Harley. Dick was a slightly balding custom house painter in his late fifties and seemed very happy with his entry into the

H-D mystique. He carefully dismounted to display his Harley Davidson helmet, boots, socks, jersey, and reached for his H-D water bottle to freshen up. He was one happy Harley Davidson recruit. We shook hands, and he proudly showed me his array of three leather pouches, all mounted on his handlebars.

## New board members contribute enthusiasm and optimism

"This one's for my sunglasses. This one's for my garage remote control. This one's for my cell phone, and my freeway speed pass transponder fits right in my saddle bag by my water bottle."

He was one proud and happy camper. Gotta love the enthusiasm of the new guy on the block. New board members aren't that different. They come to their first meeting full of the enthusiasm and hope that they now have status and can make a difference. They just can't wait to get home to their spouse and share all their accomplishments. Oh, yes, Dick did pull out his digital camera and insist on pictures. This was an event that would recur every time we stopped, be it for gas, the Mexican Federales, or just lunch. Dick was going to have a record of this event. He was our scribe.

## Detail-oriented planners have their place

Alongside Dick was Les. Les was riding the single most popular bike in America, the Harley Davidson Heritage Soft-tail Classic.

For those of you who know, I need not say more. For those of you who don't, you wouldn't understand anyway. Les is a successful mortgage broker, also in his late fifties but with swept-back blondish hair going a bit to gray. His helmet had the look of pure shiny chrome and shaped like the head of the *Alien* creature in the Sigourney Weaver movies. He was slick. Later on in the trip he would have the opportunity to explain to me in excruciating engineer-oriented detail how he and his brother had managed to retool the exhaust and the fuel system to squeeze eighty horsepower out of a V-Twin powerplant meant to put out just sixty-five.

"Les the Mortgage Broker," or "Les TMB," had two other bikes in his collection and pointed out that he really needed two more to satisfy his needs. Les TMB was an experienced rider. He had never been to the Mexican Baja but had carefully planned our route from Irvine to the Mexican border. We would have only three or four miles on the freeway and the rest on beautiful winding mountain roads on the Ortega Highway to the Anza Borego Desert on the other side. He had his maps but had left his bifocals at home, so he couldn't read them.

Les TMB was an extremely meticulous planner who had a great respect for detail. I am not. The fact that we got lost three times on the way down did not escape me. It didn't bother me either. I was just there for the ride. One mountain road was as good as another. But you do need planners on your team. You need people who are dedicated to details. You just have to be ready when all those plans and details don't work out exactly the way they are supposed to. They never do, but that's life on the condo board as well as in the Baja. But you need those guys.

Wild Bill pulled up about twenty minutes later, as promised. Buddy Jeff was following him. They both drove big old Suzukis, famous for dependability and speed. Most grizzled H-D riders refer to them as "rice rockets," or "crotch rockets" for the more colorful. Jeff was having an electrical problem, the bane of any motorcycle, be it Milwaukee Iron or Japanese.

## Deal with the unexpected and move on

We didn't get much time to meet Jeff except to see a wonderful smile that showed all thirty-two white teeth. We were late and needed to get going. Jeff's Suzuki then broke down again just five hundred yards down the road. We left him with instructions to swap for Wild Bill's daughter's bike and to meet us down in Ensenada for dinner. We left him on the corner of Jeffrey Road and Irvine Boulevard. None of us expected to see him again. Sometimes you just gotta move on.

The three hundred mile trip down was fairly uneventful, except for the three miscues in directions previously mentioned. No big deal really. We stopped several times for gas and a beer and got to know each other a bit. All three of them wore long pants, long sleeves, and leather boots. Les TMB had a stylish denim jacket. I wore shorts, a T-shirt, and an old pair of Jack Purcell sneakers. They had saddlebags filled with rain gear, change of clothes for three days, power bars for interim sustenance, and who knows whatever else. I had a skinny nylon zipper pouch with two pairs each of underwear and socks. My toothbrush was in my back pocket with my Lipitor. I took a fair amount of good-natured abuse in regard to my manner of travel. Truth is the next day, three of us were in shorts and T-shirts. Les TMB didn't give up his denim jacket.

## Crisis #1: insurance

When we got to the border at Tecate, we faced our first crisis. Wild Bill and I walked up to the little hut where you buy Mexican insurance. You really need this, not so much to protect your bike but because if you don't have it and get in an accident the Federales will throw you in jail. We've all heard stories about Mexican jails, and nobody was interested. So Bill and I paid our $23 for three days' worth of coverage and got $100 American changed into pesos for the trip. Dick and Les TMB were distraught. They wanted to get comprehensive insurance to protect against theft. It wasn't available, but it's barely even available in America. Bikes are just too easy to steal, and the premiums are about 30 percent of the bike's value. To me, it's just part of the risk. Not to Dick and Les TMB.

Their bikes each cost about $30,000. Dick's was just a week out of the showroom. Bill and I sat at the border crossing for twenty-five minutes while the other two went from building to building, trying to find additional insurance. Who could blame them? Well, it wasn't to be. Bill explained to them that the place we were staying at in Ensenada was a great seaside resort that had a huge twelve-foot wall all around it. The actual parking area was a good mile inside the grounds, and there were security gates along the way. This was one safe place. Not to worry.

"But what about the second night?" they lamented. Well, we had no reservations for the second night, but we planned to make it back up to Mexicali, another border town, and we could always just cross back over into Calexico on the American side for the night.

"Oh well, I guess we'll go," Dick said, but not before calling his wife on his cell to check in and tell of his quandary. "Yeah, we stopped to get insurance. But not enough. No, Hello? Hello? Honey you're breaking up."

## The need to know: full-disclosure or not?

Bill and I wildly waved our arms and made motions for running our fingers across our throats and for hanging up. Dick didn't get it. This was not 'need to know' information for the wife at home. It would not enhance her weekend. Kind of like when you decide what you're going to tell the rest of the condo residents after a tough board meeting where the news is not good. The choice is full-disclosure all the time, or maybe a little discretionary silence when knowledge will not enhance the overall neighborhood ambience. Maybe wait till the crisis is over and then tell the full story? We each had our own perspective. Dick had a right to his, and he exercised it. He would pay the penalty.

Sometimes when you're faced with a serious glitch in that new roofing project that threatens to cost an extra $10K or a problem with the landscaping that might mean you have to dig up and replant the back forty, you have decisions to make. Do you really need to let every neighbor know every step of the way, or is your obligation to inform them when the ifs become realities? Open governance is a popular theory. It is not always the most efficient or effective way of doing things. There are some extreme possibilities that are not always essential to share. A guideline might be, "If they can't do anything about it and it's not yet final, let's see what hard information we can share and what conjecture we should keep to ourselves."

We crossed the border. Three yards down the street, I stopped to remove my obnoxious, heavy helmet that the state of California had required me to wear. Talk about lifting a weight off your shoulders. I won't go into the conflicting theories on the benefit or detriment of motorcycle helmets. Let's just say I was the only one to stop and take mine off. The others just stopped, waited, and said nothing. That's the nonjudgmental part. Sometimes you just have to do what's right for you and let other people do what's right for them. Nobody wanted to hear or give any sermons.

The rest of the way down to the Estero Beach Resort, just a few miles beyond Ensenada, was uneventful. It just kept getting hotter, an easy 115 degrees by midafternoon. Bill and I paid for everybody's gas because, in their frantic quest for the unobtainable insurance, Dick and Les TMB forgot to get dollars changed into pesos. We pulled up to the twelve-foot-high walls, as advertised, went through the security gate, and drove down to the main hotel area through another security gate into the parking lot by the bay.

## The glue: you need those kind of guys

We just about fell over. There was Jeff's Suzuki parked by itself. We were whooping and hollering in amazement. We found Jeff out by the veranda bar on his third margarita with the remains of a huge platter of real Mexican nachos. He had his thirty-two-tooth grin on and was just as happy to see us as we were to see him. He had stopped at a dealership in Lake Forest, got the electrical problem fixed, and took the coast road straight down to Ensenada. It was actually about two to three hours quicker than our mountain route, and riding the coast isn't such a bad a choice. Same goal achieved, different route, another good lesson for a condo board meeting.

Five very happy campers. We swiftly caught up with Jeff in the margarita department and were all asleep by 9:45. In that short two hours by the bay south of Ensenada, Jeff proved to be the Mr. Nice Person of the group. The wonderful smile was backed up by a personality to match. His warm fuzzy style of communication brought us all even closer. A pat on the shoulder, a playful poke in the ribs, and an easy laugh made the road ache disappear. The Cuerve Gold Tequila probably helped too. Jeff had been down to the Baja with Bill dozens of times and even knew some Spanish that he artfully employed with the waiter and service people who had the same warm reaction to him as us gringos. When you have a group of five individuals with different agendas and different styles, you absolutely need a guy like Jeff that just adds the social glue no matter what the challenge. His communication skills brought everybody together. His reward was to bunk in with Wild Bill, whose snoring was prodigious. But never a complaint from Jeff, who just rose about a half-hour later than the rest of us, trying to recoup the sleep he had lost the night before.

The next two days were filled with riding through the Baja desert in heat that climbed too high to describe. Back in Irvine, they were in the midst of a heat wave that brought the temperature over a hundred. You can just imagine what it was like in the desert. Or maybe you really can't. Jeff's gas tank held only two gallons, 90 miles worth, while the rest of us had driving ranges of between 125–250 miles. We stopped as needed for Jeff with never a complaint. On one 115-mile stretch between San Felipe and Mexicali, Jeff had to flag down one of those famous 'Green Angel' emergency vehicles to siphon some gas to get him to the next stop. Jeff was not the planner that Les and Dick were. He just relied on providential good luck and was never disappointed.

The detail of the trip was in the riding. We would generally cruise down the straight two-lane highway of the desert at a steady 80 mph. Les TMB and Bill were the speed demons of the group. Les's Soft Tail was tricked out to do 158 mph, and he proved that frequently as he blew by me like I was parked. Bill would be second to nobody and was usually ahead of Les. They would always be waiting by the side of the road, way up ahead. When Dick and Jeff and I caught up, we'd all admonish each other on the importance of staying together in the desert, and then Bill and Les would blast off again.

Nobody broke down. We just went at our own pace. When we climbed into the mountains with the tight S-curves and switch-backs, signs warned to reduce speed to 20 mph. I would drop down to about 35, and Wild Bill would accelerate up to what seemed like 68. He would lean into those mountain hairpins till his bike was barely 30 degrees off the pavement. I spent half my time looking over the side of the road for a 'Bill Stain', but he was always waiting for us by the side of the road, about twenty miles ahead.

I have never encountered any human being with driving skills at that level. He was a big idea man with the courage of his convictions and a great leader for the adventure. Les TMB and Dick were the planners and worriers. Les TMB had style. Dick had humility. Jeff was the unifying force that brought comfort, and I ended up being just a bit of a curmudgeon.

It was the last day heading back. Les TMB and Bill were discussing what route to take because the route Les TMB had planned once we crossed the border seemed to have disappeared, and without his bifocals he couldn't find it. We all had driven about twenty miles north into the cooler mountains when Bill blew by and signaled me to pull over. We had to turn around. We were not on the planned route through the scenic part of the mountains. It was cooler, not scenic. I liked the cooler part, but I followed along back down the mountain onto the desert floor where the temperature was hellacious. We sat in a group in the sun for nearly twenty minutes while Bill and Les TMB discussed alternatives with Dick and Jeff. I didn't care one way or the other. I just wanted to go. And in fact, after twenty minutes of getting nowhere, that's what I did.

"I'm heading that way." I pointed. "If you guys decide it's wrong, then somebody come and get me. You drive way faster than I do anyway, and it won't be a big deal. I will not sit here one second longer watching my skin blister and suppurate. I'm outta here!"

I fired up my scooter and got into the wind and some level of comfort. Twenty minutes later, Bill snapped by me in a heartbeat with Les TMB not far behind. Apparently the road I had taken was acceptable after all, and we continued the trip. So my single contribution to the adventure was to break the stalemate that kept us going nowhere. I didn't plan. I didn't know. I just had the confidence that after forty years of bike riding all over the country, I would not get hopelessly lost and would eventually find my way back home. What I also knew was that we could still be sitting there in the desert sun, listening to the detailed, meticulous planner try to reach agreement with the big picture adventurous single-minded guy. Dick would go along with whatever decision surfaced, and Jeff would make everybody feel good about it.

My contribution was to take action, any action, and know that things would work out one way or the other. You need those kinds of guys too. Don't you?

There is one final lesson to be learned here. We drove through Mexicali at the end of the second day on our way to spend the night across the US border so Les TMB and Dick could be happy with the insurance situation. We passed several beautifully big resorts with huge walls and security gates. But we kept on going to get to a Best Western in the United States with no security at all. We stopped and discussed the options. Here I made another contribution, or tried to.

"Why not stay down here in Mexicali with what looks like good security? If we stay in Calexico at the Best Western, you'll be insured, but it's a border town with a huge record of auto theft and no security. Chances are much better that you'll get your bike stolen there and not here."

"But at least there we'll be insured," said Dick and Les TMB.

"But here you won't need to worry because it won't get stolen at all," I repeated.

They wanted to cross the border. They would rather play to lose. I actually didn't care that much from a practical point of view. I drove an old '79 Low Rider with over 400,000 miles and sufficient oil and road grease covering it. It was barely recognizable as the classic old Harley Shovelhead that it was. Kind of like my own little antitheft device. Much better than LoJack. No self-respecting bike thief would even give it a second look. At each roadside rest stop when we finished razzing Dick about all his Harley Davidson decals and constant phone calls to his wife, he would take his turn and ask me, "Now what year was it that you last washed your bike?" By the way, we stayed at the Best Western in Calexico.

We all did fine. We made it to Julian by midday on Sunday, had the obligatory apple pie and ice cream, compared our Lipitor dosages and cholesterol counts, and mounted up for the home stretch. It had been a great trip. I am certain I will never choose to drive through the Baja in late spring again, but we are planning a trip to Big Sur or maybe Taos in the fall. I'd ride with those guys again, although bottom line was that poor Dick lost his bowling privileges for three weeks. Full disclosure – a good idea or not?

Coming back along the Ortega Highway is always pleasant. It's a beautiful road with home as the destination. A stop at The Lookout is customary. Just a ramshackle snack bar sitting on the edge of a scenic gorge with a big dirt parking lot and plenty of benches, picnic tables, and boulders to sit on and look out over the panorama with thirty or forty scooters parked in the lot. The crowd is a mixture of graybeards and manicured cell phone yuppies who wear full leathers in the summertime. Nobody seems to be too judgmental. The graybeards do a lot less chattering.

The five miles leading up to The Lookout is a wonderful winding two-lane just a tad wider than much of the rest of the road, and you can really fly. You're heading uphill, so with the throttle wide open, you can maintain great control. Passing slower traffic is no problem, and most everybody on the highway is courteous and pulls just a foot to the right to give you an easier time. Well, most everybody. The five of us blew by an old pickup that decided that today was not a pleasant kind of day and moved to the left just as Les TMB was passing him. Les is a skilled driver on a fine motor and made it by him, but not without a quick juke to the left into what could have been oncoming traffic, but wasn't. I was close behind and passed on the right as I saw what was happening. No harm, no foul. We heard the guy's horn complaining behind us. He tried his best to stay on our tails.

The Lookout loomed ahead, and we slowed to enter the crowded parking lot. Bill went in first, then Dick, and Jeff right behind. Les and I slowed to let the path clear. Les pulled through, and I followed. Just as I left the pavement and hit the dirt of the parking lot, that asshole pickup truck came roaring into the lot, cut right in front of me, and tried to grab a space that wasn't there. I grabbed my front break, stood on my rear brake pedal, and went right down with 750 pounds of Milwaukee Iron on top of me.

The bike fell to the right, and for the first time in forty-three years, I was under it with the hot exhaust pipes branding my entire calf and upper thigh with what I'm told is 1800 degrees of hot blue steel from my twin exhaust pipes. Adrenaline is a reality, and I guess it was that wonderful chemical that gave me the strength to push the nearly half ton of machine up and off me within about two to three seconds. The pain of the burn has about a half second delay before it hits your brain and then rapidly becomes meaningful. With both hands, I pushed the bike up with such force that it went over on the other side. I got up, lost my balance, and fell right back down on top of those very same pipes. Right on my ass. It burned through my jeans in a millisecond and seared right into the fat of my butt cheeks. I leaped up as quickly as I could, slipped, and fell again, right back down on those same pipes and then just rolled off onto the ground. You've probably seen those restaurants that advertise Mongolian Bar-B-Q, well this was Jewish Bar-B-Q.

It all took less than eight seconds. The driver of the pickup leaps out of his cab and starts screaming at me for driving so fast up the mountain road and passing him and I deserve what I got and worse. He was a skinny, tattooed, greasy-haired low life with a mean look and a loud wise-ass mouth, and I just lost it. Maybe it was still the adrenaline. I felt the pain in the background being crowded out by my own rage. I whipped my helmet off, grabbed it by the strap, walked up to his loud ugly mouth, and rapped him upside the head with my helmet as hard as I could and then hit him again and then again. He went down, and I hit him again square in the face with my helmet and took out his nose. He wasn't shouting anymore. In fact he was pretty silent. I had given him a solid kick in the groin while he was on the ground. Then I dropped my helmet, grabbed him by the shirt and his greasy ugly hair, and dragged him three feet across the dirt to my bike and jammed his bloody face right onto my lovely hot pipes.

He then began to make some noise. It was a guttural shriek as beautiful as you would ever want to hear. I picked his head back up off the pipes and shouted something and took the greatest joy in smashing his face, lips first, right back down on the pipes, generating another extraordinary sound of agony. I cauterized his bleeding nose – no extra charge. Right in the middle of this, I got hit on the left side with a flying tackle that knocked me off the skinny SOB. Bill thought it was enough and felt the best way to end the incident was to hurtle his 310-pound frame at me rather than trying to discuss alternatives. You need guys like that.

I picked myself up. Looked at my leg for the first time and began to feel the onset of the pain. I went back to my bike that was still lying on its side and managed to get it upright. I kicked out the stand, let it rest, looked it over, and got my breath. I felt a thread of nausea wandering up from the pain and realized there was quite a crowd all around. My instincts told me it was time to leave. I took a deep breath in through my nose, swung my sautéed right leg over the saddle, hit the starter button, and heard my ride come to life. Nothin' can stop it. I kicked it into first and slowly pulled out of that dirt lot and onto the pavement. Then I was doing sixty in a second or two with the wind in my face and the pain introducing itself to my brain explaining in its own subtle way that we were going to be in for a challenge. The most uncomfortable part at that moment was my ass. My leg was in the wind with nothing touching it. My inner thigh was also pretty much in the wind with no contact. But my ass was on my saddle, and it hurt. Really hurt.

A couple of minutes later, Bill came whizzing by doing about a buck twenty and signaled me to pull over. I like Bill. I really do.

## ... marbles ...

I respect Bill. You just have to. But I didn't pull over.

I don't know why. I still don't. I was riding, and I was good and I didn't want to do anything but ride. Ride home. My mind wasn't really functioning in its normal rational mode. I was fifty-eight and had just done something violent, for the first time since '69, back when I was a combat medic. Violence tends to put your psyche in a different gear. Can't explain. If you've been there, I don't have to. If you haven't, there's no use in trying. But I think I've used that phrase before. Sorry.

Bill pulled in front of me and slowed down to my speed. Les came up alongside me next and signaled to pull over. Then Dick and Jeff were behind me. I pulled over.

"You all right?"

"You better take a look at your leg. That's nasty."

"Naw, I just need to get home. Let's go."

"You'll never make it. That's a bad burn. You need to get to the hospital."

"I'm going home."

"Bub, you're being crazy. You need to take care of that. It will get infected. We need to get you to a hospital."

I had spent a great deal of time in my ugly youth at Fort Sam Houston. I had been assigned to the burn unit at the Brooke Army Medical Center where all the kids returning from 'Nam who had encountered massive applications of napalm were treated. I knew a lot more about the treatment of burns than I wanted to. They were right. I needed to clean it out. I had been rolling in the dirt. I had to debride the wound and clean it out.

That was the right thing to do.

Les checked his map. "There's an aid station three miles up the road. It's where the forest rangers hang out. Let's stop there. They must have first-aid stuff."

"Okay, lead the way." Les pulled out first. Bill pulled out alongside me. Dick and Jeff tucked in behind us. We got to the aid station in just a minute or two.

Nice guys they have working there. Firefighter types. One was younger, maybe twenty-six or twenty-seven. The other was in his mid-thirties. They seemed to know a little about first aid, but in fact I knew more. I let them take my vitals and then used their equipment and cleaned out my calf and thigh, but I really couldn't do much about my ass. The younger one was saying I should put on a dressing. He was wrong, but I was polite. The older one insisted they transport me to the hospital. I refused.

"Your pulse is 180 and your blood pressure is bottoming out. You're in shock. You don't know what you're doing. Hey, guys, can't you do something about your dumb old friend here? This isn't right."

They made me sign a waiver with Bill signing as witness and then started telling me again how I was in shock and how the pain was really just starting and in an hour it would become so bad that I'd faint and go off the road and on and on. I shook both their hands with a sincere smile and walked back to my Scoot. Bill and Les were starting to question me and convince me to listen, but they know how I get. Bill followed me all the way back to Irvine. Les, Dick, and Jeff decided to continue on the more scenic route through the mountains and got home about three hours after Bill and me. Bill never left my side until I pulled into my driveway and then he went on down to Sav-On to get me some spray antiseptic. He looked me square in the eye and got a coherent smile and a wink and he was off.

"Call me if you need anything."

"Keep the rubber side down!"

I had about two hours before my wife would be home. This was not going to be easy. I got myself upstairs and swallowed three left-over Vicodin from an old out-of-date prescription. I took the garden hose and did a better job of cleaning out the burns and dropped my pants to do what I could with my ass. It was not only difficult to reach back there, but the stretching really aggravated the burns on my leg. I knocked down 1000 mgs of Ibuprofen and found some of that Bactine kind of spray to act as a topical anesthetic for the burned area. It didn't seem to do much. With my limited knowledge, I sat out in the backyard with the hose on a slow trickle just keeping the wounds irrigated.

The pain was beginning to muster its forces. Pain is a chemical thing. It's all in your head, just chemicals sending messages to your brain. That's all. You have to hold on to that thought. Another thought crept in there that said, "Maybe I should get to the doctor and get an updated prescription of Vicodin or something."

Two hours later, my life's partner breezed in from shopping with the girls.

"How was your trip?"

"Great, really great. Mexico is something else."

"Why are you watering your leg? What the hell is that? What did you do?"

It was clear that I was all right. That was the most important thing. She had to see that I was all right and able to chat, and it was just one of those little things that seem to happen to me. Not to worry.

"What the hell happened to your leg? Are you crazy? We need to get you to the hospital!"

"Calm down. It's just a burn. It'll be okay. I've done this a million times before. It will heal."

"You've never done that before. I can see the muscle. Are you crazy? Look at your thigh! You have a hole in it! We need to go to the doctor. Right now!"

"Honey, I'm fine. Go in the house. Just let me sit out here and relax for a while. It's Sunday. The doctor isn't there anyway. Just go inside. Please."

She did. It was about 3 AM before I realized that I would definitely be going to the doctor some time very soon. I used up all the old Vicodin and chased it with an Ibuprofen and Zantac cocktail. I did that every two to three hours and managed to hold off passing out. I lay in bed on my left side and really had trouble getting up, so I had to bother my poor bride to keep getting me damp face cloths and ice wraps. She didn't get much sleep either, but she's a gem. She didn't say one more thing about doctors or hospitals. I guess she knew I knew.

At 7 AM, she got me into the car and over to the doctor's office. They took me right into a treatment room. The doctor looked at it and explained the difference between first-degree burns, second-degree, and third-degree. I had a good selection of all three. The good news was that second-degree burns have already burned through the nerve endings, so the pain is nonexistent. It's only the first-degree burns at the edges that hurt. They really hurt. He said I had to go over to the Anaheim Burn Center to see a specialist, but that's another story.

He gave me a new prescription for the pain and special dressings and a tub of silver nitrate. Great stuff that silver nitrate. He left shaking his head, and one of his nurses came in to dress the wound. She was young and pretty and made an audible "ugh" sound when she saw it. There was just a tinge of fear in her eyes, and a greenish hue appeared under them. She swayed a bit on her crepe-soled white nurse shoes. I told her I would be happy to do the job, just hand me the materials and scissors and stuff and I could handle it.

"Are you sure?"

"Yeah, sure. I've done this hundreds of times."

In fact, I had, just not on myself. I did need her assistance with my ass. But we handled that last, and she was getting more comfortable and secure. I didn't hurt her a bit. She smiled and thanked me and kind of suggested that it would be nice if I didn't tell anybody that she assisted instead of doing it. She was young and cute, with long auburn hair and a great smile.

I said, "Sure."

Getting up and on my feet was quite a chore and would be for the next four to six weeks. Skin has a lot of important functions.

One of them is to kind of hold you all together in a nice envelope. When you tear a large portion of that envelope, two things happen. The rest of the envelope gets pulled in unusual ways that are actually quite painful all by themselves. Second, your skin is a major source of insulation for your body. When you lose a large part of that, you get very cold. It was over eighty degrees outside. It was the summer, but I was freezing with constant chills for most of the next month.

The recuperation was fairly uneventful. The great and wonderful doctors at the Anaheim Burn Center insisted on surgery because so much of the underlying skin had been burned away. They told me without it I would be looking at a six-month recovery period and have major scarring and disfigurement. I chose not to listen to them and was back on my Scooter in six weeks with only modest scarring that is now all but invisible. Silver nitrate is a remarkable substance that promotes healing in a magical way. Keeping yourself clean, changing the dressings every four to six hours, and keeping somewhat flexible, as painful as that is, seemed to be the right formula. I knew what I was doing, and it was my body anyway. The last thing I wanted to do was get into a California operating room.

By the way, I never did beat the crap out of that guy in the pickup. I should have. I really should have. But the truth is I just stood there glaring at him while he shot his mouth off. Then he kind of looked down at the dirt for a minute, looked up, and apologized.

But I wish I had.

# Letter from Tel Aviv

## Frontiers of mortality/morality

### Thursday, September 30, 2010

*Today is Shmini Azeretz (really).*

*A very full day awaits. I was picked up in front of my Rabin Square condo by my Sabra cousin, Dafna, in her little Volkswagen Golf. Cheryl, my other cousin, also visiting from America, was already riding shotgun. I got the entire backseat to myself, not bad at all really.*

*The goal was Yavne'el and Tiberius, both just below Lake Kinneret (the Sea of Galilee). It would normally be a two-hour ride. Tel Aviv is right on the coast of the Mediterranean, the west side of the country, about midway north-south. Lake Kinneret is all the way up in the northeast, bordering the Golan on the north and Jordan and Syria on the east.*

*We began the drive passing very large cities on a major highway heading northeast out of Tel Aviv. The land is flat, allowing you a visual of the entire expanse of the cities as they stretch out for probably six to twelve miles into the distance. Keep in mind that Tel Aviv is a major big city, and the suburbs are proportionate. If you were in Boston, think Newton, Brookline, or Wellesley. The interesting thing is that they are all Arab cities and nothing like what I saw in Jerusalem. These were mighty fine cities with well-to-do people living their lives. No tumble-down buildings or anything marginal in a socio-economic perspective. You knew they were Arab because each one had a very tall minaret and mosque visible in the distance, the largest buildings in each city. These are the pockets of Israeli-Arabs that are the underlying long-term concern of the Jewish Israelis who want to insure that this remains a Jewish state.*

*The three of us discussed the Arab's proximity and living together. It's really quite simple, with very little confusion. It's very much a comfortably segregated society, especially if you're Jewish. Everybody keeps to themselves, except when it comes to commerce. There doesn't seem to be any overt animosity. At least, not from my cousin Dafna.*

*By the way, she is sixty years old, a geologist, an elementary school teacher (five days a week), a lover of nature, a part-time children's zookeeper, and a very gentle lady who took part in the Six-Day War when she was twenty-two and each subsequent war, as did most everyone in the country.*

*The population in Israel has an emotional, psychological, and physical involvement in the IDF (Israeli Defense Force) in* striking contrast to our own United States of America. To be simple, everybody cares but is not obsessed here. It's a very normal and accepted part of life. It is a country at war that is now enjoying an extended period of remission. The last time the United States was actually in a legitimate war that threatened our existence was World War II. Even then it took place an ocean away on either side. This is different. Very different.

Outside of Israel I've heard there have been major headlines about the current efforts at peace talks. While in Israel, at least to the many people I've been in contact with, it hasn't come up once. When I've asked, I got shrugs, like I was asking about some obscure butterfly flying by. Everybody here seems to 'get it'. There will never be peace. It's just about as likely as GM developing a 100 mpg car. Maybe they could figure it out, but nobody's investing in it. After all, there never has been peace here. Almost never.

## Now back to my day, sort of.
## It was about to become a good one.

The discussion in the car continued about the Arab cities. The main point that came up was that if you're an Arab and want to build something in one of the Arab communities, you have to go through the normal permit process that you would in any American town. There are zoning laws and building permits and everything that you expect, along with the usual red tape *that bureaucratic governments embrace. On the other hand, if you are a Jew and want to build something in a Jewish town, it's about as difficult as putting a quarter in a vending machine and having all the permits just pop out. If any Jew wants to build anything, that's a good enough reason to have it built. No red tape. No nothing other than the kind of stuff for which Olmert is under indictment.*

*We're not talking about The Settlements or East Jerusalem. We're talking about just normal, undisputed Israeli territory. This is about the only place in the world where the construction business is booming. My buddy Bart Brass, an emigre and old fraternity brother, circa 1966, told me that the 'National Birds' are those huge yellow construction cranes that you see at the building sites of every major high-rise building. I've certainly traveled around high-growth areas in our country, but I've never seen such a consistent sight as I do here. Everyone is building something all up and down the country that I've traveled in. I have not been to the Negev yet.*

*But just to put a point on that last part. The Arabs are 100 percent clearly second-class citizens. And that's just the way it is. There's no pretense about it. And there doesn't seem to be the overt hatred that should go along with that. I'm thinking about the Jim Crow American South during the first half of the 20th century. The history books showed that we experienced a whole lot more active violence like the Ku Klux Klan, scattered lynchings, and a very active attitude that "kept the black man down."*

*It's not really like that here around the cities. Everyone
keeps to themselves in their communities. There are plenty
of wealthy Arabs. They get the shaft every time they try to
deal with the government, but they do govern their own cities
without incident. Call it segregation, apartheid, or any of those
other words we've all heard. The anger and vitriol seems to
be focused in Gaza, Jerusalem, and The Settlements. Even
along the West Bank, there are very little visible problems.
During the day, we stopped many times at restaurants and
other places, and there wasn't the slightest feeling of tension. It
was nothing like Jerusalem. People smiled and interacted with
each other without incident or overtone 98 percent of the time.
I'll tell you about the 2 percent at the end of the day later.*

*I think I could compare it to Boston during the 1950s.
We were always identified as one of the most racist cities in
America. I always thought we were just a city of neighborhoods
that pretty much kept to themselves. There was Chinatown,
the North End, South Boston, Newton/Brookline, Beacon
Hill and Back Bay, Roxbury/Dorchester, Dover, and Weston.
I don't have to explain the ethnic and cultural unity that each
one of those names evokes. We began having violence when
Judge Garrity insisted on following federal law by integrating
the schools. Having ethnocentric communities can be a
very peaceful way of life, as long as nobody is forcing people
to interact with others who are different and making them
nervous. Dafna was very clear about the less than equal
treatment the Arabs got, but she showed not even a little*

animosity. They were them, and we were us. As long as she wasn't dodging bullets, as she did during the first Lebanese War, everything was fine.

I'm really trying to give you a travelogue kind of story here, but the politics is as much a part of this land as surfing, shopping, and cosmetic surgery are to Southern California. It's tough to ignore.

After traveling about thirty minutes, we made our first stop at a kibbutz. A good friend of Dafna lived there, and Dafna had asked whether I was interested in what a kibbutz was like. I gave her an enthusiastic, "Yes." So here we were.

We pulled through the gate and drove in on a road that was sometimes paved and sometimes hard-packed dirt, passing a row of about twenty house trailers. Dafna explained that the people who lived in them were not part of the kibbutz. The kibbutz had decided to rent out some of their land to let those people live there. It was unclear who they were or why they chose to live there. Living can be expensive in Israel, and it just may have been an affordable option for those people living on the outskirts of the kibbutz with no involvement as well as a welcome source of additional rental income for the kibbutznicks.

We drove along the winding road past quite normal-looking houses, normal in that they had two or three bedrooms in the smaller homes with yards. They didn't look at all like a US neighborhood because there were no fences or walls or even property lines that are often marked by shrubbery. The homes

were well spaced, if not irregularly placed. There would be two
or three close by, and then you would drive a hundred yards
before another, and then around the corner another. Very
random. We pulled up to the house we were heading for. A lady
who looked to be in her fifties, wearing jeans (not designer
jeans) and a plaid blouse, was kind of diddling around with her
tree in the front of the house.

We got out of the car and WHAM – Phoenix, Arizona-style
summer heat. If you know what I mean, I don't have to explain. If
not, ask somebody from Tempe or Mesa. Riding in the
air-conditioned car was fine. Getting out was not. Israel is a
very hot country. The further inland you move, the hotter it
gets. It was physically painful. My skin hurt. The heat is
constant until the sun goes down. I was the only one who was
really bothered by it, and I was really bothered by it. It was the
end of September, but it's more intense during the summer.

After making a mental adjustment to this furnace, I did what
I could to interact. That was also an ongoing barrier more
formidable than the heat. Everybody spoke Hebrew, even my
cousin visiting from Brookline. In the car we would speak
75 percent English for my benefit. But when we visited any
place, it got kind of weird. It was a very long day, and it became
a little disconcerting. People were very nice and occasionally
explained to me what they were saying. Frequently, they would
engage me in limited conversation with the English they all
knew. But there was just no reason for five or six people who
normally spoke Hebrew to try and carry on a conversation in

*English just because there was an old bald guy from Boston there who didn't speak Hebrew.*

*The tree; the lady began hitting it with a rake knocking off some ripe fruit. It was a guava tree. I had never seen a guava tree, and I bet you haven't either. The fruit is about the size of a large lemon or an elongated plum or peach. The skin is wrinkly and has a texture thinner than a tangerine and slightly thicker than an apple or pear. You eat the skin. I took a bite of one that was handed to me, and it was quite mild tasting. The flesh was a pale yellowish white. The flavor was not nearly as intense as the guava juice you get in Albertsons. The fruit was apparently not quite fully ripe, but tasty. The nice lady gave me another one, which I ate. This was my only error of the day. I had skipped breakfast and only had a huge cup of coffee I made in the condo from a French press that I didn't know how to operate. Half of it was intensely strong, half very weak (I actually had two cups), and it was black.*

## Now back to the kibbutz

*The three ladies chatted away in Hebrew. I stood politely just looking around. This would be the norm for the day. The most important point is that I like just looking around, and I have a skill level of minus 3 when it comes to small talk and a minus 8 when it comes to female small talk. Sorry about that.*

*It was not the classic Marxist commune that you might picture, but it had its distinctions. It was a farming kibbutz.*

*That's important. Also realize that real farms are really big. Lots of land for as far as you can see. It reminded me of the Amish farms I saw outside of Indianapolis. Indiana is very much farm country. Not the mega-farms owned by the agri-giants, but we're talking hundreds and hundreds of acres. This was a community of about 200–250 people supported by farming.*

*We walked through the village area and first came upon the laundry building. There was one good-sized single-story building of roughly 1300 square feet and three rooms. To make it simple, there was one lady who was in charge of doing all the laundry for everyone in the village. She had two or three ladies who would help her at various times. Simple. Imagine living your life and never worrying about laundry. I thought that was cool. We also drove by a garage. They took care of their own farm equipment as well as all the personally owned automobiles. A few people worked at the garage, and that was there job.*

*Dafna asked me if I had ever seen a house built of hay and would I like to? We drove a bit farther up a little path, and Dafna was mostly correct. This was the deal: A young couple in their late twenties with a baby of about eighteen months was building on a three-room addition to the wife's parents' house. It was not a house 'built of hay'. It was an addition with a cement foundation, normal interior sheetrock walls properly finished with an exterior layer of plaster, and then eighteen inches of hay being used for insulation with another layer of limestone, mud daub, or something very much resembling stucco. There was a latticework of thin strapping boards* built around the whole house to keep the hay in place and about fourteen inches of gravel at the base for drainage and a corrugated metal roof.

A few days prior, most of the neighbors had all come over to help with building the walls, breaking the hay down from the bales, stuffing it into the latticework, and applying the exterior coating. When we got there, the husband, his brother, his father-in-law, and his wife were all outside doing more work on finishing the exterior walls. They were elbow deep in this mud-daub/stucco, limestone, and plaster mixture and applying it with their hands to the sides of the building. It was just as messy as you would expect. The woman's mother stood in the doorway holding the toddler and chatted with us.

The husband was one of three brothers. One of his brothers was there helping. The other had moved to the United States. He spoke perfect English. Yes, they had licensed professional electricians and plumbers who did all that kind of work. The foundation was professionally poured. Most house-building work doesn't take a lot of highly skilled labor, just one person who knows what he's doing to direct the others in what is menial and simple work. They had built lots of houses in this kibbutz, and most people knew from experience what needed doing. They took care to do it properly.

The idea of hay-insulation was new to them. This couple was ecologically minded indeed, and thought they'd give it a try. This was not one of those 'green' communities of the future, just a couple who felt they wanted a better-insulated house.

## ... marbles ...

The inside of the house had a kitchen with stainless steel appliances that you would find in the United States, with a nice range hood suspended from the ceiling. It had nicely tiled floors, not Travertine, but new and delightful. It just happened to be on a kibbutz, and it just happened to have a lot of the labor supplied by their neighbors. It was their family's responsibility to get the job done. It may be that there would be another communal work session where twenty to thirty people would join in, but maybe not.

As I spoke with the husband, I got good feelings about what life was like. He was not at all condescending but did express some mild amusement at my questions. All I knew about kibbutz life was what I had read in books, both in school and later in life, about the early American attempts at communal living. Then there were the attempts at Utopian life-styles in 19th century America reborn as the hippy communes in the 20th. None of this really seemed to apply. I got the feeling that this was just a community much like any other. They had a central laundry; you just didn't have to pay for it. There was a garage where your car got fixed, but there was no bill. There were knowledgeable, well-trained people handling the work on the autos and farm equipment, but that kind of work does not require ongoing turnover of highly trained technicians. Fixing an engine, once learned, is pretty basic. Some of us are better with tools and using our hands than others. Sometimes there's a problem to get solved, and it gets solved. There was nothing 'cultish' about this place.

160

# ... marbles ...

I saw the central daycare center. All the kids went to public schools outside the kibbutz, but they had day care for the preschoolers. I was told that early on in the development of the kibbutz, many of the younger children actually slept at the daycare facility, but not anymore. They all still had breakfast together. The whole community had lunch together, and it seemed like dinner was sometimes communal and sometimes not. There was no evident rigidity. They had a basic style and philosophy of living that was reasonable, practical, and flexible. They adjusted to whatever realities presented themselves. I think that's why they rented out the space to the people in the trailers. The community needed some additional funds for something they all wanted.

I watched about seven or eight children aged six to fourteen practicing for a little community show they were going to put on to celebrate Shemini Atzerat. There was a little stage built in the field. Everyone was smiling.

We spent more time there chatting. The lady we came to visit was a little upset that we wouldn't stay longer and have a glass of cold water with her in her living room, but we were just at the beginning of our day and had to get going.

This kibbutz was not some kind of weird group of society rejectionists. All was normal, just organized a bit differently. I think the biggest difference might have been what was missing. I don't think anybody there was worried about their 401k. I don't think any of them had any grand dreams of acquiring outsize wealth and living a life of idle splendor. They lived in normal houses with reasonable comforts and amenities. They all worked very much as we do, just at a different pace and with different priorities. Farming is not an easy life, I am told. But it's what they all had chosen, other than the laundry ladies, the daycare ladies, the mechanics, and maybe some communal cooks. I'll bet there was even a bookkeeper somewhere. And if that didn't suit them, then they left, as had the young homebuilder's brother. They were there by choice.

There was no doubt they were working hard at finishing that house. But they had plenty of help. The building materials were bought by the kibbutz. You need to think about how similar their lives are to ours, not the differences. I'm not sure what happens to the elderly or infirm. The kibbutz was only about forty years old, so there didn't seem to be a geriatric or 'aging in place' issue. I have a feeling that the older people would be taken care of. What was missing was that overriding drive for the accumulation of wealth. There seemed to be a much heavier focus on today, tonight, and Simchas Torah that was coming up Saturday.

By the way, Israel is not a heavily religious place. There are customs and cultural traditions, but other than in Jerusalem, and the fact that most businesses close down for the Jewish holidays, there's not a lot of God stuff going on, although I'd say most of the restaurants are kosher. The ritzier ones in Tel Aviv are clearly not. They serve shellfish in abundance. Jewish is more of an undertone as a religion. It's more of an Israeli nationalism that is obvious.

## ... marbles ...

*Off we drove out of the kibbutz. I didn't pay much attention to the road, as I was dealing with a very unhappy stomach that was getting more and more unhappy. I'm not going to go into the next difficult two to three hours, but just remember that all I'd had in my stomach was about sixteen ounces of strong black coffee and two not quite ripe guavas. The time was spent in the backseat of a VW Golf with two ladies who liked to ride with their windows barely cracked open in the heat I described with the AC on. My tummy was very upset. The only plus was that I am highly resistant to motion sickness and stomach upset of most kinds. But this was just a stupid combination of circumstances, and I spent most of my time focusing on the famous 'Mr. Spot' on the floor with my sphincter clenched and quietly groaning to myself on every exhale. I was in the backseat, and thank goodness nobody noticed. We stopped later on for lunch, and I recovered. Not a problem thereafter.*

*We did drive by the Plain of Megiddo – Armageddon, if you're unfamiliar with the Hebrew. It is a very beautiful plain with a few rolling hills in the distance. A 'Tel' is an archaeological dig, a small raised mound of earth. According to Dafna, 'Tel Megiddo' is actually 100 yards, corner to corner, where they have uncovered different layers of civilization. It was a great find for archaeologists, but there are scores of them all over Israel with more yet to be discovered. In fact, they had closed this one up and it was not being actively worked. There are only so many archaeologists to go around, and I guess they were really needed at some construction sites where new buildings* were in mid-erection. As the contractors dug down to create the foundation, they kept coming up with scores of artifacts. The Israeli government is strict about trying to identify and preserve that kind of stuff. There's a lot of work for archaeologists in this part of the world.

Just as a side note, it's kind of strange listening to a lady in her early sixties speaking broken, but understandable English in that lilt and style of a Jewish grandmother who would be telling bedtime stories to her grandchildren. Then you realize she is explaining some very technical geological and archeological events along with a high level of awareness of the ecologic problems. I was talking to a person who had a master's, if not a PhD. It was difficult to get attuned because of her style of speaking. The overt contradictions in this land really made you stop and think, especially when she was telling me about her multiple wartime experiences as a young girl, a young mother, a middle-aged mother, and most recently as a grandmother. She was still participating just like everybody here does. I think that is the hardest thing to try and explain.

There is a focus on reality here that is foreign to most Americans who have a mall-based reality or a Wall Street-based reality. At first, everything seemed quite foreign, odd, and disconcerting. It still is. But there are pieces of real life that shine through. When you realize it, you realize everything we are missing in the States. Not that we need war on our soil or excruciating heat and taxes that you would not believe. Life here has some jagged edges of reality to it that you can't fully grasp.

## Take a minute's break here with me

*When I was in Jaffa and then up north in some Arab towns, you really do hear the call to prayer five times a day. It's broadcast over extremely powerful loudspeakers from the mosque. They are quite serious. I think that might be it. People really take their lives seriously here. They focus on what seems to them to be the important things. They have movies, theater, museums, opera, the arts, sports, and all of the distractions and entertainment that we enjoy, but it seems to have a more appropriate place in their lives.*

*It's not that they don't 'party-hearty' and really embrace their recreation. There was a huge festival in Rabin Square right outside my windows last night, and the police were dancing along with the people. No kidding. It wasn't like at home where the LAPD or the OC Sheriff have a malevolent, unsmiling presence aimed mostly at intimidating potential troublemakers and keeping order. I couldn't believe it. There were probably three dozen police for a crowd of about 4000 with a big stage and loud music, and so many of the police were just joining in. And those that weren't were smiling and laughing. The law enforcement folks have some serious stuff to deal with, but they seem to know the difference. They are not interested in creating trouble where it isn't, just to show how tough they are. Everybody is tough here, and there's not much need to flaunt it.*

*We passed Megiddo, and both ladies wanted to stop for something to eat. They kept asking me if I wanted to stop for* coffee. I politely said no. But they were hungry, and when we came upon a sign that said 'Switzerland', we laughed. Dafna knew where we were. Do you know about the town north of LA called Solvang? It's kind of like a little ethnic retreat of what I think is Swiss or Dutch or some kind of Baltic/Nordic people. Well this was something similar. I'm not going to get the spellings at all right, so bear with me.

Dafna said to me, "You like kreplach?"

"Of course," I said. No matter how ill I felt, I wasn't going to lie. And my stomach was starting to level off. At least I wasn't getting any sicker, and getting something solid in me seemed like a good idea. This was the community of a Russian sect called Circassians. I think they may have been related to the Caucasus, but with all the different Hebrew, English, and Cyrillic spellings on the signs, I couldn't be sure. It was definitely a Russian community of some sort.

We drove around and saw the incredibly neat streets and unusual homes built with black (basalt) brick, some whitewashed with limestone to become white. There was a mosque at the top of the hill that was a checkerboard of black and white. Dafna emphasized how much pride they took in cleanliness. The streets were swept by everyone, every day. We stopped in at a restaurant and got two large platters of kreplach, one cheese and one meat. See, no kosher concerns here. That and a large pitcher of ice water was our lunch.

We started with a small plate of two different kinds of cheese. One was very much like a smoked gouda. Next to it

were slices of something like leumi. It's a white goat cheese
that Dafna pointed out was not really as ripe as it should have
been, a little too moist and not salty enough. There were three
slices of each, and we ate them. Then came the kreplach and
a dipping sauce that is called labane'e (forgive my phonetic
spelling). I recognized it as something I had been served
many times in Jerusalem with my breakfast. It's white with the
consistency of yogurt and the taste of lemon chiffon. You like? I
did. It's not a bitter lemon, but a sweet lemon, mild and smooth.
So I dipped some of the kreplach in it, and then just scooped
out some on the pita that is always served everywhere, and
always warm, soft, and puffy. It is a sin to think that they sell
stuff in America and call it by the same name. There is no way
you can understand how delicious it makes anything, and it's
served with everything.

Then Dafna got a little twinkle in her sixty-year old eyes and
asked, "You like a little something sweet?"

Sweets aren't at the very top of my personal list of likes, but
eye twinkles from sixty-year-old Israeli female war veterans
with broken English are another thing entirely.

"Of course!" I said. "And maybe a little mint tea?"

She told me what she was going to order. It sounded like
nocki, but it wasn't. I asked her to repeat it twice more and then
just gave up.

They brought us two plates of a confection that was finely
shredded dough, like the consistency of Shredded Wheat, only
very, very soft and gentle, not that sticklike texture you get with

real Shredded Wheat at home. Inside was a very sweet and
warm cream cheese filling with crushed pistachio nuts on top.
There were four pieces about one inch square on each of two
plates. I wish I could describe the texture of the dough because
it wasn't anything like dough. They were more like ultra skinny
velvet threads woven loosely together. They just looked like
little bales of yellow hay with green crushed nuts on top and
soft sweet warm cheese inside.

Yes, they were very good. I had two pieces and let the ladies
really indulge. I'm also really getting to love sweet hot mint tea.
By the way, there are two different types of mint. I never knew
that before. We always have 'hard mint' back in the United
States. It's all I've ever seen. Here they have something they
call banya. They say it is soft mint, and the leaves are flat and
look like basil. At first I thought that's what it was. It does have a
softer and gentler mint taste. You know how sharp mint can be
in something like peppermint? Well, this is the opposite. It was
gentle mint, kind of like the labane'e was gentle lemon. It's not
really important. I just thought I'd mention it.

We left and drove around the town again. We finally got
back on the road just after noon and headed up to Yavne'el,
our actual destination. We saw the signs that we were getting
closer, came up over a rise, and there it was. In truth, you've
seen it before if you've been to Tuscany or driven through the
Blue Ridge Mountains or come upon any farming valley. You're
offered a wide vista of regularly shaped fields of various crops
of different colors, some already harvested with just red earth,

others in the middle of harvest, and some untouched green. Dafna had tears inching down her cheeks.

"I can't help it," she said. "Some people love the sea. Some love the mountain. I love this land and the fields."

That was a good thing. I wish I'd had my camera, but cameras have not been made to capture such sights. It was a pleasant and beautiful farm valley. It was probably the least unique part of the day, but it was no less beautiful because it exists in many places, made all the more beautiful by the tears of this lady who truly loved it so freely. This was where she had grown up.

The village itself has about 2000 residents, most of them farmers. This is not a kibbutz, just a farm town. It was geographically about the size of Holliston (plus all the fields) with about a quarter as many houses and much smaller streets. We went to Dafna's parents' old house that was now being rented to tenants who clearly did not appreciate what they were living in. Dafna said they were 'naturists' and commented that they often wore no clothing. But more importantly, they didn't water the olive trees, fig trees, or other fruit trees. The trees were still alive, but the fruit was suffering and so was Dafna. She stopped in to say a quick hello. We stayed in the car and then out she came.

We drove over to her brother's house. His name is Dorin, and he owns a building materials factory with a partner. He is second-generation ownership. His father, Nechemya, now passed away, started the factory with another man as partner.

# ... marbles ...

Dorin now ran it with that man's son and said that the other man's sons would take it over some day as his own son had no interest. He was quite proud of his daughter, Keren. She is apparently a very big music star in Israel. He showed me the plaques from two gold CDs she had earned. He gave me a copy of her latest and insisted that I Google her and see how famous she is.

Dafna confirmed all of this, though without the bursting pride of her brother. She felt he and his wife were kind of 'riding the coattails' of a celebrity daughter and maybe had lost sight of the more normal world. He had a nice house. When we pulled into the driveway, my cousin Cheryl jumped out and dragged me over to this big date palm in the middle. We started picking and eating dates right off the tree. She really loved this, and I can't blame her. They were delicious. She had many childhood memories of visiting Israel, and this was one of her favorites. Understandable.

I could describe the house and furnishings to you, but I'll just say that it was a nice big house with too much furniture, archaeological artifacts, modern art, and 'stuff'. Dafna's husband is a professional fisherman and fishes with nets. When they fish for shrimp, they drag the nets along the bottom of the Mediterranean and pick up a tremendous amount of pottery from old shipwrecks. This house was filled with it. The condo I'm staying in is filled with it, and I'm sure the best examples are in Dafna's own house. They can certainly be interesting, but there is such a thing as too much. Each piece loses its specialness.

## ... marbles ...


Dorin and his wife were entertaining their own guests when we got there, people of the same age. They had just returned from a trip to California, Seattle, and Costa Rica. Even though there were the usual language issues, they made it pretty clear that they were rich. The only parts of the conversation I understood was when they mentioned dollar amounts, and it was always "A million here makes five million there" and "Why not? Land in Costa Rica is cheap – lots of Americans are buying and visiting." I felt like I was back in Orange County. I was sitting in what was supposed to be a 'million-dollar house'. Somebody was trying to impress me, or themselves. Not so much.

I did enjoy talking to Dorin when he spoke English to me. He had three children and a dog I bonded with immediately – no language barrier. Dorin looks physically fit and friendly. He took my e-mail address so he could send me to the website kerenpeles to see just how famous his daughter was. I gave him modernmusiclessons.com.au. We'll see what we'll see.

It was a nice visit. We spent over an hour with about ten minutes total in English. We piled back into the VW and drove around town a little bit as Dafna and Cheryl reminisced. Cheryl had made several trips there when she was young, and Nechemya was quite the character. He was said to be a very big man and even bigger in personality. Quite a brawny and aggressive sort who carried a pistol in the glove compartment of his truck. After all, this was Israel of twenty years ago. He had spent more than a night or two in jail for brawling. The story they liked to tell most was when he got in a fight in a bar and knocked out three teeth from an Arab he didn't like very much. When he came before the judge in the morning, the judge fined him 20 sheqalim for each tooth.

Nechemya then supposedly said, "If I knew they were that cheap, I would have knocked out all of them." Whereupon the judge doubled the fine and sent him home.

Nechemya was my grandmother's brother from her father's second marriage when he returned to Israel without my grandmother's mother. But we needn't go into that saga. I'm just trying to give you an orientation as to how 'extended' this family is to me. We headed for the Golan. It was about 2 PM. I wish I could have met Nechemya.

•••

Now, I'm going to take a break from my typing to get lunch. Dafna told me that the best falafel place in all of Israel is right across the street from me, so that's where I'm heading ...

Okay, maybe Dafna thought it was 'the best' falafel in Israel because the guy made it with four falafels. In Jerusalem, it's a standard two. Then when I got here to Tel Aviv, I got a couple with three. Now I get this huge one with four. It was good, but the balance with all the other condiments seemed to be thrown off. They did have a self-serve bar that let you add more of whatever you wanted, but I didn't bother. I know a place outside Dizengoff Square I'm definitely going back to. They have that special lemonade.

•••

## ... marbles ...

When you see the Golan Heights there is no mystery about its strategic importance. There is no way Syria is ever getting that piece of property back.

Oops, I forgot about Lake Kinneret and the River Jordan. I'll do us both a favor and make it very brief. Lake Kinneret is a huge lake that is the largest body of water in the area. Just look on a map. It is also known as the Sea of Galilee and is a big Jesus thing. It was the water he was supposed to have walked on. There are a ton of Christian holy sites all over the place. This is the Galilee where he preached. The Jordan River runs from Lake Kinneret down the Jordan Valley to the Dead Sea. We did get out twice along the Jordan River, and, yes, I did go down to the water's edge to wash up a bit. It was not quite a baptism of any sort.

Just across the river was a campground where there were a few hundred tents set up. The river was full of happy people frolicking about in the water on their rafts, some fishing. Where I was it was not a very wide river, maybe thirty yards across. A little river with a big reputation. We stopped at the spot where John the Baptist was supposed to have baptized Jesus. Very big tourist attraction. You can imagine. They still do some ritual baptisms there on special occasions, and, yes, they do sell little bottles of 'holy water' in the gift shop for 6 sheqalim (about $1.65).

We drove all around the sixty-mile circumference of the lake, a good part of which was up into the Golan where we went in and out of Jordan many times and through a piece of Syria. No

173

guards. No checkpoints. The only way we knew we were in and out was that our cell phones kept going off as the service changed from one country to another. I asked Dafna how this could be. I thought this was a real problem spot. What, no border guards?

She said very simply, "Nobody wants any trouble, so nobody makes any trouble. Because if you make trouble, it's big trouble. And nobody wants that."

The Golan is an incredibly high cliff with a huge plateau encompassing square miles that are now all farmland and grazing land developed by the Israelis. It's a very large butte, or mesa. This is where the beef cattle graze. I also saw lots of banana plantations and endless fields of one crop after another. My cousin Cheryl went on and on about how when it was all Syrian land, there was nothing there except a bunch of Syrians who would sit on the mountain and shoot down at settlers. And now look at all the wonderful things the Israelis had done. My cousin Dafna was a lot less boastful.

"We did what we did, and now we have it. It would take a lot to give it away. I don't think that will happen."

Then she told us a story or two about her service there during the first Lebanon War when Syria joined in. She had been a bus driver transporting troops from there to Tel Aviv and back again. Her story was rich with detail that made you feel what it was like to be doing something that seemed as mundane as driving a bus. When filled with bone-weary soldiers who were dazed, injured, or worse, it took on a different tone. She did that for about two and half months, *although the actual fighting didn't last more than a week or so. I think that might have been the Six-Day War, or the Yom Kippur War. There were just so many I had trouble keeping them straight. And what did it matter anyway?*

*It reminded me of a chapter in Catch-22 when an old Italian woman is weeping at the bedside of a bandaged-up soldier who she thought was her son Giuseppe. She was moaning and groaning over him with her husband and other son. The soldier was actually Yossarian who was told to just lie there and shut up and pretend, because Giuseppe had died a week ago and the family had traveled all this way just to be there with him. And the other son finally tells the wailing old woman that the soldier in the bed isn't her son Giuseppe, so she should stop wailing, and the mother said, "What difference does it make? He's dying!" I don't know if you recall that particular chapter, but I thought of it when I was listening to Dafna's war stories.*

*What difference did it make which war? There were so many, and will be so many more. I think maybe that's what Joseph Heller was trying to say too. But better not get me started on Catch-22. Remember 'The Soldier Who Said Everything Twice'? Oy, I won't go there.*

*We drove through the Golan for more than an hour on the same kind of road that runs through Positano in the South of Italy and PCH along the Big Sur in California. Except in California it's kind of straight. This was nothing but hairpin turn after hairpin turn. At some you had to stop to make the switch back.*

175

It was beautiful country, but there was a sixty-year-old lady driving who had been driving since eight that morning. Then we had to make a U-turn. Cheryl was literally screaming. I would have too except my throat went dry. Of course there was no guardrail or shoulder of any kind. It was insane. But these were some of the roads she had driven her bus down forty years ago. She didn't laugh or smile or say anything. She just drove and told us stories about how there used to be deer that lived on the Golan when it belonged to Syria, and the wolves had traveled in packs and eaten the deer.

Then the Israelis captured the land and began raising cattle. The wolves realized it was a lot easier to raid the herds and eat the young calves that couldn't run or fight. Then the settlers would stand guard. They would put out piles of poisoned meat to attract the wolves away from the cattle. The wolves would eat the poisoned meat. They would die and then great flocks of vultures and certain types of eagles would come and eat the dead wolves. Then they would die because the wolves were poisoned. Now the eagles and vultures were almost extinct because they had all been poisoned by mistake.

Once there was a problem because the eagles were eating up all the little mice, voles, and other creatures to feed their eaglets. Apparently, they only laid one egg each year and we're in danger of extinction – the eagles, I mean. The eagles were dying out from the poisoned wolves, and the population of small animals was growing out of control. And it was all because the wolves had decided to eat the calves instead of the deer. She pointed out that it was very important to be very careful when you started poisoning animals, any animals. You never knew where it would lead. She told us stories about snakes and scorpions, and even though she was very frightened of them and had seen the pain of a scorpion sting, she respected them all.

She is a special person. One who cries at the sight of open fields of crops and transports soldiers back and forth over a 100-mile route day and night. Her father knocked out someone's teeth in a bar brawl without a thought, and her mother cooked the pigeons that her brother shot in the fields. During one of the wars, she brought her little zoo of animals up to the caves where the little children were taking shelter to help keep them calm while the rockets were dropping.

As we walked through the fields or people's yards, she told me the names of each plant in Hebrew and then tried English. She broke off pieces of the plants to make me smell and taste them. She knew those fields like I know Albertsons. There is a balance to her that is quite attractive and comforting. She accepts the strange world of constant conflict that she lives in. Her husband is a professional fisherman who is at sea five days a week and comes home for Shabbos and heads out again on Sunday night. He was the little smiling old man who met me at the train station with the keys to the condo. He was home for the High Holiday season, ten days in a row. He was the one who collected all the old pieces of pottery.

It was getting to be about 4 PM, and the sun was starting to come down.

# ... marbles ...

*Did you know that Israel passed its own Daylight Savings Law that sets the clocks back a full month before the rest of the world? They did it for religious reasons so they could get started with the High Holidays sooner and be done with them sooner. I'm not sure why that was important. But Israel is one hour ahead of the rest of the world for four weeks a year. This just started in 2009.*

*It was getting dark. We were still on this ribbon of a road, and I was eager to be on the way home. But we still had things to do.*

*One of them was unexpected. We came around a sharp corner, and an older lady was standing on our side of the road. Her car with her husband at the wheel was on the other side, and if you didn't know what the word 'distraught' meant, all you had to do was look at this woman's face. She was between fifty and sixty. Her husband looked older. They looked lost. We stopped. She had an extended conversation with Dafna. We were at a point in the hills where there was no cell phone reception. Good thing they were not broken down, just lost.*

*Dafna tried to tell her how to get 'found'. When we left, she thanked Dafna and trudged across the road to her husband. Dafna told us that they had become lost, but the husband wouldn't stop to ask directions. So now they were really lost, and it was getting dark and they were both getting pretty scared. That was easy to understand.*

*"I just hope the husband listens to her," said Dafna. "It will be dark soon, and they have two to three miles to go and a few turns to make before they get back to a main road."*

# ... marbles ...

All three of us looked back out the window and watched them pull back onto the road. I'm guessing the guy had the good sense to follow the directions Dafna gave, if only his wife could remember them all. Aside from going over the edge of the mountain, they wouldn't know if they were going over the edge in Israel, Jordan, or Syria. But I guess that wouldn't matter quite so much. Kind of like Giuseppe.

The good news is that just as the sun was setting we were indeed coming down out of the Golan. I will spare you all of the gasps of awe that came from Cheryl and Dafna when we came out of a turn and saw the beautiful expanse of the great Lake Kinneret. It seemed to impact them a lot more than it did me.

The sun set right over the tip of Mount Hermon, which in fact does have a tip. Then I really did wish I'd had a camera because for a long moment the giant orange globe was sitting right on the tip of the mountain, like a ball balanced on a fingertip. It would have been one of those photos that could sell a million copies. The sun continued to sink lower behind the tip of the mountain, and darkness fell. I think there's a biblical expression about 'darkness falling on the face of the deep', or something like that, but the good news was that we were back on a main road and saw a sign that said Yavne'el was just twenty kilometers away. We were on our way back!

I didn't bother describing Tiberius to you. It is a seaside resort. That's all you're going to get from me. I didn't describe the oldest cemetery in modern-day Israel that we stopped at or the remains we encountered. And I won't. I will tell you that we entered D'Gania, the oldest kibbutz in Israel at 101 years, drove around the inner circle of traffic, and watched them set up a huge stage with sound and lighting equipment that would have suited the Verizon amphitheatre in Irvine. The roadies looked just like the roadies in the States. Dafna wanted to be sure I had the chance to see everything that could have been important to me. If I had wanted to dally, we would have. I didn't, so we didn't.

We headed south past Yavne'el because before we could stop for supper, we had to stop at her sister-in-laws for an appearance at a special Bar-B-Q. Her sister-in-law's husband had just been named mayor of a small Arab village nearby, and the elders were coming up to their house to pay their respects. Yup, this Jewish guy was being welcomed as mayor by these Arabs. Go figure. I guess he was a good guy.

We arrived and there were about six or seven large circular tables set up in the backyard. Each table would seat about ten, but the only people present when we got there were their two sons, two nephews, two daughters, and the sons of a neighbor lady who was there to help serve. There were more than a dozen platters of food all set out in a large outdoor Bar-B-Q area with a medium-sized fire already burned down to the point where the coals were gray. All the kids were between eighteen and twenty-one, and all in the army and home on holiday.

They looked very fit and handsome as they were introduced. One was a paratrooper, one was a combat engineer, one was a tank commander, and one smiled shyly and couldn't really tell us what he did. But the others all treated him with a lot more respect, and it was explained to us that he was part of a very 'special' group that was quite secret. Even his parents didn't know what he did.

I'll take a second to mention that the country is filled with youthful people of this age. They all look like professional athletes, but not the bulky kind, the sleek kind. None of these young adults smoke or drank. They were all very polite, but not obsequious, more respectful. They laughed a lot and would kid each other with little pats on the shoulder and pokes. The girls would join in too. They were also in the army. Everyone between the ages of eighteen and twenty-one is in the army at some level, just as soon as they finish high school. The only deferments are for kids that want to go to medical school, but that is very rare. Most will go into the army for three years and then go on to some kind of further education for usually three years. And many will return full-time to the army for a period of years. Like all Israelis, they are in the active reserves until they are fifty years old.

Bart Brass told me that only about 30–40 percent go on to what we would consider college. Many of them go into vocations. Those who go to the more traditional college finish in three years, not four, because they just don't take as much time off. They are more mature, ages twenty-three to twenty-five, and know why they are in college. They want to learn what they need and get on with their lives. There are plenty that go on to get their master's and doctorates. There are many scholars and academics in Israel. The only exceptions to this pattern are the extreme orthodox, but they are another problem entirely. They are quite a bad problem, similar to any group of 'fundamentalists' whether they be Christians, Muslims, or any religious right-wing extremists. They hold an unreasonable amount of influence for all the wrong reasons.

The town elders came along with their wives shortly after we arrived. The women were in traditional dress, not burkas or anything like that, just the normal headscarves (jihabs) draped around their shoulders and tightly framing their faces. They brought gifts of flowers and fruit. Our Israeli host, hostess, and neighbor were dressed in typical Israeli garb, khaki shorts and tank tops. The young boys and girls wore long pants with black T-shirts with their army unit or division logo on the chest. God they were handsome.

But the reason I am telling you about this is that it seemed so meaningful to me in this place where all you hear about is strife and war. That's the way it's always been and probably always will be. Here was an Arab village welcoming a Jew as their mayor. Here the elders came to pay their respects, and they brought their wives. This was not just an economic practical business thing. This was a genuine cultural exchange with presents and well wishes between people of such radically different orientations. They were sharing an evening together with family and children, even though the 'children' were soldiers prepared to rejoin their units just as soon as Simchas Torah was over, or sooner if they heard a siren. These were individual people and families who understood that they were living together, and they were doing the best they could with that situation. And you know what? It wasn't so bad. There were platters and platters of food, hesitant smiles, and respectful nods that grew into a laugh from one of the men and a hand on a shoulder and more laughter. The women were much more reserved, but now they were all smiling and the kids were passing the food. More of the townspeople showed up. You could tell by the way they dressed.

Dafna's sister-in-law begged us to stay. Dafna asked if I wanted to, but I said no. I think I had gotten the best of it. This was not my place or my party. But to see it was certainly my privilege. This was not Netanyahu and Abbas and Hillary filled with pretense and politics and bullshit. If there is ever to be a solution, it will not be a one-state solution or a two-state solution or a set of Oslo Accords. It will be a few townspeople getting together with their families and food and respect, and yes the children will be there ready to go to war because, if they weren't, there might not be this gathering.

As we were driving away to yet another adventure, we talked a bit about how lovely it all was and how impressed the neighbors were with Cheryl's ability to converse so well in Hebrew. We spoke just briefly, at least Dafna did, about what could possibly be the solution to all the wars and all the problems. I offered that I didn't believe there was an obvious solution at all. If there were a solution, we would know it because most everyone really wanted one. But what I thought

and what I think is that the solution is not in 'making a peace'.
We always think of 'doing something' to create a solution. In
this case, I think it's the opposite. I think it's the 'not doing'.
What artists call 'negative space', the yang to the yin.

If we could just get rid of the haters, the rest of the people
would be fine. There are so many haters and ready-to-be-haters
primed to explode on both sides that things just can't settle
down long enough for any kind of real coexistence. Every
insult is blown out of proportion. The Jews are so afraid of
losing the Jewish State. If they do, they believe they will be lost
as a people. Certainly there is some truth to that. You look at
Judaism in America, and it doesn't seem to be the same as
what's going on in Israel. Israel is truly a nation that is Jewish.
But it is a nation whose primary goal is to protect the Jews of
Israel and to offer an enduring sanctuary to the Jews of the world.

It's not a bad concept if you're Jewish. But anti-Semitism
exists, and the word 'virulent' was invented to describe it. It's
been around as long as the Jews, and it's not going away soon.
But somehow we need to get rid of the haters on both sides. If
Hillary could have been at that Bar-B-Q, I think she would have
understood. Maybe she already does and just can't do anything.
After all, she did lose to Obama.

It's getting close to 6:30, and we need supper. Apparently
Dafna knew all along where we would eat. There was an
excellent Arab restaurant just off the highway behind a gas
station. Cheryl knew of it too and was getting very excited as we
got closer. It was night now, and we were still more than ninety

minutes from Tel Aviv. Despite my love of all things that begin or end with the word 'food', I was just really beaten down and tired and wanted to go home already.

Not to be.

Thank goodness.

We parked and went into a large bright white room with rows of tables with paper tablecloths. There was a large buffet-style setup at one end with six red-shirted, young, and modern-looking Arab men franticly spooning things onto small plates. There were around twenty items on the buffet plus a huge bowl of assorted olives. By huge, I mean the bowl was almost three feet across and eighteen inches deep. There was another big stainless steel bowl about the same size just being filled with something I didn't recognize.

Dafna, Cheryl, and I walked over to the large buffet and just looked. I started recognizing things. I had been in the country more than two weeks and had paid attention. I recognized all six of the dishes I had shared with Bart Brass when he had taken me out to eat, and there were twelve more. Some were recognizable as types of salad. Almost all were cold except for a huge stack of stuffed grape leaves that I would later find out were warm.

Dafna asked, "So what would you like?" and laughed.

Cheryl laughed too, and we sat down while Dafna spoke to one of the young men who was scribbling madly on a little pad of paper.

No, I am not going to go through everything that we ate.

# ... marbles ...

Dafna had been carrying a camera with her all day and snapping photos here and there. She asked one of the guys with the red shirts to pose with me with fourteen empty dishes all balanced along each of his arms and me in the middle. We were both smiling.

Quickie: In Hebrew, printed on the back of all the red shirts, were the words 'My back may be facing you, but my heart is with you'. Kind of cool, huh? Arabs? Maybe not so bad.

You already know all about the bread. I'll say again it is 100 percent essential to everything. They served lemonade, but not with mint. There was no alcohol, in case you didn't already know that about the Arab customs. We had skewers of lamb. This was my second consistent experience with skewers of meat. Don't bother. This is not a country that has good meat. Their lamb and chicken is like the quality of our American pita bread. Why bother? It's tough and fatty and unnecessary. This land is a vegetarian's dream come true. Cheryl tried to make a nice comment about how good the lamb was, but she was just being patronizing. I acknowledge that I've focused all my eating on local eating places, no haute cuisine so far. Maybe if I go out and spend $50 on a meal, I'll get good meat. But why bother? None of us had any room for dessert, just mint tea and a single bite of something like baklava, but wasn't.

One final event. While we sat eating, another group of younger folks sat down nearby. One of the young men, according to Dafna, said, "You sit over there. I'll sit here. I don't want to sit near any Arabs." Dafna tsked.

# ... marbles ...

When we were done and finally leaving, Dafna went right over to the young man and said (I got the translation after), "Do you have any Circassian friends?"

"Yes," he said. "I play football with one of them. We're buddies."

"Well those people over there are Circassian, not Arabs. You can tell by the head scarf the woman is wearing."

"Oh."

"And did you know that the Circassians serve in the Israeli IDF, the same as you?'

"Um, yeah."

"Yes, they all do. They are Israeli too, you know."

I was close by Dafna, though obviously I didn't understand the words. I just looked at the faces. Dafna's calm gentility. The young man's respectful interest and the slightest bit of embarrassment at the last words. Dafna never said a thing about his comment. She knew enough that she didn't have to. And the young man knew too. We left.

All I could think was what that scene would have been like in America. The mental image made me sick. We've lost our kids.

We dragged ourselves back into the VW Golf and headed back to Tel Aviv. I'm not going to relate the quiet spotty conversation for ninety minutes. There was nothing essential except that Dafna handed me her own personally printed-out recipe for shakshuka, which was that marvelous egg dish that I had flipped out over. Apparently, it's a very common breakfast item. She makes it all the time. It's extremely simple to make, and should you darken the doorway of my kitchen once I get home, you can be sure I will put a pan together with only a nod. Just give me three hours warning to let it simmer properly. I also got the names of two other dishes that were just wonderful. I can go to the Persian market and ask for them from the guy behind the counter. I've also learned just a bit about goat cheeses that I can put to good use.

And today is only Friday.


xx

oo

bb

# Woolloomooloo lunch

## False frontiers of the Golden Age

ENJOYED A NICE LUNCH with a seventy-five-year-old neurologist from South Africa named Ron Joffe. He's the father of one of the ladies I work for at the museum, and kind of a 'museum' experience for me himself. He told me what it was like growing up in apartheid and how in his early teens he knew it was not a country where he wished to live. That makes a bit of a statement as to who he is today. He did grow older, marry, and have two children there, but he moved in the '60s to London (lived on Abbey Road!), back to South Africa for a few years, then to Australia in 1974. His wife was a pathologist and one of the first to specialize in cytology, a cutting-edge branch of medicine at the time. She was one of the first in Australia.

I had met Ron and his wife at a small dinner party at his daughter's home. It was a very comfortable group of ten that included my son and Shannon, his soon-to-be fiancee. Ron's wife was there and appeared to be in the early to mid stages of dementia. They were on the cusp of placing her in a facility that could better meet her increasing custodial needs. She was competent enough to attend the dinner, neatly dressed and clutching her handbag to her chest, wandering about the room, and making some offhand unrelated comments. She acted perfectly respectably but created a certain air of heightened awareness and tension in her daughter, though Ron seemed to carry on. The few phrases she spoke were kind words directed at Shannon or another guest. Though her words were without context, they were simple expressions of kindness. There's something to think about.

In my lengthy luncheon with Ron, her situation came up a few times. Ron did not dwell on it. Being of an age where we can look back over the various challenges life put before us, he acknowledged it was one he had been unprepared for. As a physician and neurologist, you might imagine that he would have been more aware of what could happen. And as symptoms appeared, I would guess that he dealt with their situation in the most loving and civilized manner.

I probably should have started off my description of him by pointing out just how wonderful it was being in his presence. We're all familiar with the term 'bedside manner' as it applies to doctors. When you take that kind of personality out of the medical environment, you have a genuinely caring person who understands how to tell his own story while showing ongoing interest in yours as well as your response to his. That's a lot of verbiage to describe a very pleasant person who is a great *conversationalist.* That's a word you don't hear so often anymore. There are plenty of great *storytellers* around, though they most often seem to be egocentric drama queens. I do have the good fortune to have a few friends who are great nonjudgmental and sympathetic listeners. Lord knows I require that skill too often. But the person who knows how to balance the conversation as well as have interesting contributions is a joy. It may be that the two bottles of New Zealand pinot noir we consumed helped.

A dish-by-dish summary of our luncheon on the Woolloomooloo Wharf is available. I enjoyed it immensely. I won't go through all the details except to say that he had made a reservation at a particular waterfront Asian-style place and happily told the waitress, "I have a good friend here visiting from America. Please just 'fix us up' the best you can, but do bring a bottle of the 2010 Wanderer Pinot Noir. I believe you have it in your cellar somewhere."

That really set the tone for the experience. He had thought enough about our lunch to have selected a very good (fine) restaurant, made the reservation, and even made sure they would have a proper wine for us. He's a wine collector and knew of what he spoke. My son, Daniel, had told me that each year, for the past two, he had made a gift to Daniel and Shannon of twenty bottles from his cellar. He offered the excuse that his collection was getting too full, and he was getting too old to drink it all. But he still couldn't resist buying up a lot that he discovered he liked. Would that qualify as an example of a generous spirit?

Ron's appearance was that of a relatively healthy seventy-five-year-old and had what I think is a characteristic British-looking lipless mouth placed at just a slight left tilt on the lower part of his face, a slash really. His head tilted in the same direction as did his shoulders, which all seemed to be consistent with a slight limp. He was anticipating a knee replacement as soon as he got his wife settled. He was every bit a left-leaning, angular person from mouth to knee. He ambled along like a ship sliding gently into port. He laughed quite a bit, just a short chuckle that would make you automatically smile in return, whether you understood exactly what he said, meant, or was thinking. It's a nice feeling to smile. And that's what he elicited, nice warm feelings of respect.

He loved and respected both his son and daughter and spoke of them in a very positive way, but not at all in the proud father bragging about his offspring kind of style. I don't know how I can explain that other than to say he spoke of qualities in his daughter that I had already experienced, and there was no exaggeration. She was what she was, and it made him happy. He laughed about his physician son who specialized in dietary issues because his son was "so enormously fat."

He said, "I have to smile when I think of him in his office larding over his chair and giving advice on healthy diet."

He managed to offer this candid critique in the most loving way. What I'm having trouble explaining is that he was able to accurately describe his children, and his love and respect came through not so much in his words but his demeanor. I began to love him for that, or maybe it was the second bottle of pinot noir that he had ordered and we had half finished without even realizing it.

We began our luncheon with a single Victoria scallop presented on a palm-sized perfect scallop shell with a solitary leaf of parsley as a crown, beneath which was some sort of very finely ground herb (ginger, I'm guessing) that at this moment I can't identify. But I am heading back to the restaurant tomorrow to find out. That one single bite was simply delicious. It's what every gourmet calls an 'explosion' of wonderful subtle flavors in your mouth. There were five courses, each quite wonderful, and then Ron asked for a 'bit of a sweet' to finish things off. The waitress brought us a trio of desserts plus an aperitif of some fruit, vodka, and mint combination over ice that I had never experienced. Of course, it was great.

So there we were two happy and mildly intoxicated gents enjoying a summer's day in Sydney. Ron excused himself to 'make a pee', managed to absent-mindedly walk right by our table on the way back, and was halfway up the wharf by the time I caught him and brought him back to our little nest. We laughed.

It would make good reading if I were to narrate the context of our long and meandering conversation. It was so interesting comparing our formative years, he in South Africa and me in Brighton/Newton, Massachusetts.

Of course we went on and on over American politics. He is a great believer in American exceptionalism, which was very much a campaign topic. I expressed my candid disillusionment in what I was taught America was supposed to be about. He pointed out the obvious and then the not so obvious. The first thing he said was that regardless of the reality of my complaints, America was still the best place there was for freedom and opportunity. The best by a long shot. You could literally do anything in America. If some chose to do things that weren't to my liking, then so be it. I sort of knew this. Then what he pointed out surprised me.

"America is by far the most charitable country in the world. You never see giving of that scale and by so many anywhere else in the world," he said. "I've spent so many trips to America walking around the hospitals and universities, and every building seems to have somebody's name on it. Americans give untold fortunes to charitable causes. And it's not just those who've made their millions, but it goes through your whole country. Even the poor give to the poorer. You just don't see that anywhere else in the world. And I've been to many places."

I thought that was worth repeating. I take him at his word. He didn't seem a person to make provocative statements just for their entertainment value. I think I'll stop here and let that thought remain with you. I could profitably spend another 1000 words describing Ron, his manner, his family, philosophy, values, and so on. That luncheon was the high point of my trip so far, and I expect it will remain so when we board the flight home. Most everyone talks about 'the Bridge Climb' as the most memorable experience in Sydney.

I met Ron Joffe.

# Daughter Lisa deals with Crohn's

## Frontiers of the pain of parenthood

"DADDEEEEE, it huuuuurts!"

It's the worst sound in the world. We've all heard it. If not exactly that, then substitute *m*'s for the *d*'s and that ought to include most of you. It's not the sort of hurt that you can handle with a "kiss the boo-boo" treatment. It's the kind that has no name, at least not right now, and wouldn't for another eighteen hours, sixteen of which would be spent at the emergency room at Children's Hospital, a long ninety-minute drive in the middle of a very dark winter night. But right now, it was just a nameless impossible-to-deal-with pain that was attacking my little ten-year old daughter. The brave one. The fearless one who always looked out for her seven-year-old brother.

Lisa was the one the bullies always watched out for, and here she lay on her bed, limp from screaming. The pain just wouldn't go away. I held her hand. I had her squeeze my thumbs with all her might to transfer the pain to me. I had her bite on a wet

195

face cloth and sit up and lie down on her belly and then roll over on her back, and just nothing would make it stop. She finally stopped screaming for a minute or two, but only because she was so exhausted that she had no more breath to even talk.

"Daddy, help me. Please help me. Make it go away. Please just make it go away for a minute. Just for a minute."

"Okay, honey. Okay. Just hold on, and it has to stop. It's just a stomachache. What did you eat?"

"NOTHING! Daddy, I didn't eat hardly anything. Just make it stop. I didn't do anything bad. Make it stop hurting."

"Okay. Okay. Now you have to concentrate. Look at me. Look at me. Look at my eyes. Come on, honey. Look up at me and hold on to my thumb. Look me in the eyes."

She raised her little head and then dropped back down on the pillow wet with tears, her black curls plastered to her forehead with perspiration.

"I can't, Daddy. I can't. Please. Please just make it stop."

"You can, honey. You can. You can at least try. You have to try. I don't know what it is, but you have to try. Look at me. Hold my thumb and squeeze hard. Lisa, look at me."

And she did. She picked up her head and grabbed on to both of my thumbs with both of her hands and squeezed with all her might. And she looked right in my eyes, and I saw the pain and knew then that I had to get her to the hospital. I had to make it stop. I was the daddy. It was my job. She had tried.

"Call Dr. Katz!"

"Just squeeze my thumb. Squeeze, squeeze, squeeze. Think

about the pain going into my thumb."

*I squeeze harder. It's not working.* "Call Dr. Katz, pleeease!"

**The doctors didn't figure out what was wrong with me quite as quickly as you might think.**

**Lisa Maddock**

Of course you know that they don't make the pain go away in emergency rooms. Not at all. In fact, they won't treat you or your ten-year-old daughter with anything until the intern gets a look and then the doctor gets a look and then the specialist gets a look and they get to run their tests and take their pictures and develop their film and have the specialists look again and again because they don't want to mask the symptoms. If they mask the symptoms with painkillers, they may not be able to figure out what's wrong and won't know what to do to fix her.

So my little Lisa was wheeled into the ER on a gurney at 11 PM and got no medication until five hours of pain later. At 4 AM, my seven-year-old son was comfortably asleep across my lap, and they gave my daughter a massive dose of Demerol even though they still didn't really know what was wrong with her or how to fix her. By 9 AM that morning, they began to figure out what was wrong with her. Now it's twenty-one years later, and they still don't know how to fix her.

**There were in fact many trips to the emergency room. There were countless tests and not enough drugs to figure out the problem and take the pain away.**

## ... marbles ...

Crohn's disease is a not-so-rare degenerative disease of the digestive system. It is a chronic, incurable disease that is corrosive in nature and can appear at any site along the digestive system, from a chancre on the tip of your tongue to an ulcer in your stomach to granulomas, fistulas, and lesions on your colon and fissures in your anus. It eats away at your tissues unless it is magically put into remission by a combination of heavy-duty steroids that would make today's NFL players back off with caution. Steroids, sulfa drugs, and a pantheon of others that try and put this monstrous disease to sleep for a month or a year or maybe two.

The physical consequences patients look forward to include a series of bowel resections, colostomies, ileostomies, and more. Back in 1983, when it first attacked our daughter, very little was known about it. Not much more is known now. There was a recent promising breakthrough in the genetic medicine area, but who knows? When the doctor told us our Lisa had Crohn's disease, we thought he was talking about something that afflicted old witches. When he gave us the brochures and we saw the spelling, we found that somebody named Crohn had discovered it earlier in the century but hadn't had time to find the cure. It also told us we should not be looking forward to having grandchildren.

*My dad used to tell me that Crohn's disease was a tiny bug living in my intestines that was munching away at them. All the medicine they pumped into my little body was to make the*

198

*bug go to sleep. I remember pleading with him, asking why the bug won't go to sleep. "Soon, honey, the bug will sleep soon."*

The disease wreaks havoc on the internal workings of victims, and what's left intact is often further impaired by the medication required to treat the symptoms. Infertility seemed inevitable. It wasn't at the top of our list of concerns back then. Just surviving beyond her teen years without having a lot of bags attached to her underwear was all that was on our minds. My wife and I grew closer. We had an active seven-year-old son, Daniel, who would also join in the family effort to survive this. It wasn't easy and still isn't. My son has his own story of dealing with a world that was running away from him.

The enormous pain Lisa dealt with receded by that first evening and early morning. The drugs did their job. The problem was that eating anything at all was going to aggravate the disease that seemed to be active in her small intestine. Any food passing through the system might set off the pain. What was happening at the time was unknowable, but the disease was causing a blockage that would flare up and then go out of control when food tried to pass where it couldn't. If her intestine ruptured and burst, she could die fairly quickly. She didn't eat for a day and then the inevitable. We were back to the ER.

The doctors sedated her and brought on the army of steroids. Within days, they had performed an operation to insert a semipermanent central line in her large jugular vein that would provide all the sustenance her little body would need for the next six weeks. She was provided 500 ml bottles of a white milky-looking substance that went directly into her IV and provided nourishment. Not a morsel would pass through her lips for forty-two days. They would provide a new bottle full of nourishment about every eight hours that would slowly enter through the central line IV. The bottles cost $500 each. We found that out one day when our Dano knocked over the tripod it hung from, sending it crashing to the floor.

My wife, Carol, and I adjusted our work schedules to always have one of us at the hospital to be with our daughter during the nonsleeping hours. We made arrangements for neighbors to help out with our son when possible. People help people. There were many days, mostly weekends, when our seven-year-old was a regular sixteen-hour visitor to the hospital along with us. He charmed all the nurses. But they were easy. I'm sure I wouldn't be the first to compare nurses to angels.

Lisa was housed on the chronic care floor. Most all the other patients had cystic fibrosis. They were all kids. None of them would see adulthood. The courage we saw in those children day after day was something we all still remember. They faced their disease, their treatment, and their preemptive mortality with an attitude that made you realize the true nature of bravery. The nurses who treated them showed a different kind of courageous resilience I could never imagine.

We began to see Lisa's illness in a much different light. Lisa felt lucky. Everything is relative. Small town living can be a wonderful thing. All the kids in her grade made a field trip to come and visit her in the hospital. Children in other grades did art projects to send get-well cards. It seemed as though the whole little town of Holliston, Massachusetts, cared about our Lisa.

We spent Christmas and New Year's on the seventh floor of Children's Hospital. The staff did everything possible to get every one of the patients that they could home for the holidays, even if they were to return in just a day or two. Home for Christmas was important. But there were still a few of us left on the floor during that time. There was no celebration. Those that were still there wouldn't know the difference anyway. The next year, when Lisa was home, we all decided to go back to the seventh floor on Christmas Eve to count our blessings and to try to do what we could for the children there. We went shopping and picked out little presents for the patients too sick to leave and for all the nurses. We arrived before midnight and left the presents by their beds and at the nurse's station. We vowed that we would come back every year at Christmas to remember how lucky we were and think of others. It was a nice thought that we didn't fulfill. Life does go on, for better or worse. Maybe this year.

We would be back at the hospital many more times over the years. Lisa dealt with her disease and the inevitable surgeries and pain. Sometimes more painful than the disease were the effects the symptoms and treatment had on her life. The steroids blew her up like the Pillsbury Dough Boy. Dark facial hair came with the puffiness and is not exactly what a preteen and then teenager really wants to deal with. But it was either the Prednisone or the pain and more surgery. Kids are kids; and as the celebrity of being a patient wore off and she returned to school, the pudginess and facial hair drew their toll of taunts and snickers. It was a difficult adolescence.

*It was interesting how people reacted to me when I was sick. I recall sitting in the front row of Miss Rocheford's fifth grade language arts class. It hurt so much I couldn't even sit up properly, and my face felt like it was always scrunched up in pain. She never even noticed. She only took note when I returned from my hospital stay blown up like a hairy Cabbage Patch Kid courtesy of all the steroids pumping through my ten-year old body.*

*I remember asking to go to the bathroom in Mr. Mazarro's sixth grade science class. Before I could even get the words out, he was loudly telling me to go and not wait for the hall pass. That was a little embarrassing. I know he was just trying to be nice but all I had to do was pee...and my whole class ended up knowing about it.*

*I suppose it was better than Mr. Hardy's seventh grade science class when I ran like hell to the bathroom to avoid an accident only to be publicly chastised for not taking the hall pass. That was beyond embarrassing. It was humiliating.*

*It wasn't all bad though. I was a guest on the Good Day TV show to share my experiences as a kid living with Crohn's and did a few interviews for clinical newsletters and fundraisers. That kind of stuff made me feel like I was able to do some good along with the bad hand I was dealt.*

*The kids in the cystic fibrosis ward stay with me in my*

*heart. I'm pretty sure none of them are still around which is almost impossible to wrap my head around. You know, I was even jealous of them when we were in the hospital. They were allowed to order take-out Chinese food while I wasn't allowed to eat anything. Perspective changes a lot doesn't it?*

*I've blocked out a lot of those memories from my middle school years. Kids are mean at that age. Some adults weren't much better, regardless of their intentions. I did my best to pretend everything was fine, which led to anxiety attacks and trips to a psychologist I didn't want to talk to. Is it irony that I am now a professional social worker?*

*Once the anxiety attacks passed, I continued to try to live my life as an upbeat and smiley girl with a fast-developing sense of sarcasm and some emotional wall building. I still believe a cure will be discovered. I live my life. Is your life painless? Neither is mine.*

Lisa became a very special person with an outrageous sense of humor and sarcastic wit. She became a very strong person with deep sensitivities. She recognized her own ongoing physical pain and dealt with it. She learned to recognize the pain of others and tried to help. She grew to be a mature adult, earned a Master's in Social Work from Boston University and did her very best to help the children and families less fortunate than the rest of us. I don't think she ever really learned to keep the "professional emotional distance" needed for long-term survival in that field. She just cared too much. But she tried.

## ... marbles ...

As fate would have it, treatment for Crohn's has progressed. In fact, it has progressed enough to give Lisa a chance to consider having a child, which she accomplished despite enormous flare-ups of the disease that made her new husband wonder what exactly he had gotten himself into. In order to get pregnant, Lisa had to go off almost all her medications. It was a decision she had to make. She decided she needed to at least try. Fertility needed a clean playing field to have a chance. It wasn't going to be easy. Flare-ups and multiple surgeries followed the reduction in meds, but she soldiered on and tried to wait it out. She was able to conceive and suffered no flare ups during her pregnancy. After forty weeks of extreme discomfort, she gave birth to a healthy baby boy.

> *It's been twenty-one years, and I'm still waiting for them to take the pain away. But you know what? There are a lot of people worse off than me. This isn't going to kill me. It hasn't stopped me from achieving my goals. I work in the field for which I've always had a passion; I have an incredible husband and the most perfect little boy. I have a pretty great dog too. These are the things that get me through the pain, now that my hands are too big for my daddy's thumbs.*
>
> *I am fortunate enough to have found an incredible partner in life who now lends his thumbs when the pain becomes too much. He had to consent for emergency surgery to be performed on me at 2 AM, six days after we got married. He waited alone all through the night. He even held my damaged intestine in his hand once the surgery was complete. Now*

*that's love! Or it's a sick fascination with the small bowel.*
*I choose the former. He's waited patiently over the years*
*through more surgeries and trial medications so we could*
*become pregnant. My sweet little Jacob arrived five months*
*ago. I recently noticed that he has been pooping a little more*
*often than he had been. I've already made two calls to the*
*pediatrician who has gently reassured me that this just*
*sometimes happens with babies. She understands my "poop*
*obsession." He's probably just teething.*

And now she took a break from being a professional social worker to be a 'professional' mom who is extremely anxious over any tummy aches that may pop up with her little son. Genetics seems to play an undetermined role in this disease. But so far, so good. Maybe this will be the year we all remember our promise to go back to Children's Hospital for Christmas Eve. It's better to be there because you choose to be.

And four years later, Lisa had a second son who she could actually breastfeed due to the rapid improvement of drug treatment that seems to be fighting a holding action against the disease. They still believe a cure is on the horizon. Lisa is back at her social work job and lives in Kuliouou Valley just west of Hawaii Kai. Not a bad place to be in.

*So the good things always outweigh the bad. You just need to*
*let go of the bad. Have I told you about my two incredible little*
*boys I wasn't sure I could have, my rock of a husband who*
*weathers these storms with me and my sweet little dog?*

# ᴳGranddaughter

### Snowstorm

Outside my window
Cotton balls of white
Thrown
  Tossed
      Tortured
They    whiz in
Every
  Which
         Way
Yet somehow make it out
   Alive,

For a moment.


Emma Flowers, eleven years old (2007)

# Acknowledgment

"There are talented teams,
and there are winning teams."

*Cody Ross, right fielder
for the Boston Red Sox, 2012*

"We shall not cease from exploration,
and the end of all our exploring
will be to arrive where we started
and know the place for the first time."

*Little Gidding
T. S. Eliot (the last of his Four Quartets)*

# Make a difference

## Informational & charitable links

**Trauma Intervention Program (TIP)**
**National office**
www.tipnational.org

**Merrimac Valley Chapter**
TIP of Merrimac Valley
www.traumaintervention.com

**Crohns & Colitis Foundation**
**National Office**
http://www.ccfa.org

**New England Chapter**
www.ccfa.org/chapters/ne

**Team Intestinal Fortitude**
www.intestinalfortitude.org

**Hawaii Take Steps for Crohn's Disease Team**
**Scars are Sexy and We Know it!**
http://online.ccfa.org/site/TR?px=1183768&pg=personal&fr_id=38
46&et=YOqLTUznCi0ifXX1G8laCw

**Adoption Choices A division of JFS of MetroWest**
http://www.jfsmw.org/adoption/

**Hawaii International Child Adoption Agency**
www.adoptionhawaii.org

**Sydney Jewish Museum**
www.sydneyjewishmuseum.com.au

**Boston Childrens Hospital**
http://giving.childrenshospital.org

Made in United States
North Haven, CT
12 January 2022

14664215R00120